# A VISION FOR MISSIONS

# A VISION FOR MISSIONS

TOM WELLS

*To Bruce & Maggie*
*w/ my best*
*Tom Wells*

*7686 Granby Way*
*West Chester, OH 45069*

THE BANNER OF TRUTH TRUST

THE BANNER OF TRUTH TRUST
3 Murrayfield Road, Edinburgh EH 12 6EL
PO Box 621, Carlisle, Pennsylvania 17013, USA

★

© Tom Wells 1985
First published 1985
ISBN 0 85151 433 2

★

Set in 11 on 12 pt VIP Plantin
Typeset, printed and bound in Great Britain by
Hazell Watson & Viney Ltd,
Member of the BPCC Group
Aylesbury, Bucks

# Contents

# Preface

Not long ago I heard a missionary say, 'A need will not keep you on the mission field. People will rebuke and repel you.'

I have no doubt that he spoke the truth. What he said agrees with what other missionaries have told us. The need is overwhelming on many fields. But that very fact can be a source of frustration. The task seems so large and the missionary seems so small. Once it is apparent that the people do not want his efforts, what is left? The answer to that question is the key to whether he keeps on or gives up.

And what *is* left? In one way or another the only adequate answer is *God*.

Some months back I talked with a veteran woman missionary to Thailand. I asked her why she had stayed all these years. Without hesitation she said, 'God's command. If it wasn't for God's command I wouldn't be there.' Some may think that that answer sounds cold and hard. The stars were gone from this woman's eyes. She had not lost her ideals, only her idealism. Neither response to human need nor the 'spirit of adventure' could have kept her at her post. Yet she had an answer. She fell back on God's direction. She was under orders, so she stayed. God had commanded her. And she is not alone in this answer. Countless others would say the same thing. 'Why am I a missionary? I am not my own. I belong to Another. I am under orders. I have God's command!'

Just here let me make an obvious point. The phrase, 'God's command', has two parts. Needless to say, the important word is 'God'. The word 'command' has its place. But God is at the forefront. It is *God's* command; that is the point. Let us go back to the missionary to Thailand to see what this means.

Suppose *I* had tried to send this lady out to the mission field. Would she have gone? Very likely not! I could have mustered my most commanding voice and my most imperious style. Would she then have committed herself to going where *I* thought she ought to go? If for any reason she had done so, sober minds would reflect on her silliness. 'Imagine!' some would say. 'Imagine anyone committing herself to heed the whims of that man!' And they would be right.

But neither would the word *God* be enough to cause her to go. Something important lies behind the phrase 'God's command', namely, *the known character of God*. Why obey God's command more than mine? Because of who God is! It is what we know of God that makes His command more than vain words. This is so obvious that I need not labour it. Our view of God – what we might call our vision of God – explains a great deal in our lives. In particular, it explains how we react to things that appear to be God's commands. If we see Him as our Lord we will act in a certain way. If we see Him only as a casual observer of our lives we will act in another way.

But suppose the divine command is absent. Could there then be a reason to carry the gospel to the ends of the earth. An obvious answer would be, 'Yes, men need the gospel. They will perish without it.' But suppose we did not know that. Would there still be reason to carry the gospel to all nations? Is anything known about God that could inspire missionary work? The thesis of this book is: *God is worthy to be known and proclaimed for who He is, and that fact is an important part of the missionary motive and message.*

Now there is an odd thing about this thesis. I do not doubt that it has often lain behind much mission work. In saying that God is worthy to be known and proclaimed for who He is, I think I am saying something that has moved many missionaries. And if I am right it has, of course, been a part of their message as well.

Yet here is the strange thing. This fact, I think, has generally operated below the level of the missionary's consciousness. It is not something that has often been said. At least I have not heard it. And that is the reason for this book. I want to say it, and I want to show that it is true. There is nothing, I believe, that could be more useful for Christians to realize.

This book also has a second thesis: *those who know the most about God are the most responsible and best equipped to tell of Him.* Among my readers will be those who think that they have found God glorious in ways that other Christians have overlooked. There will be those whose motto is 'Let God be God!'; men and women who have decried the 'shallowness' of much modern Christianity. They long to call us back to a deeper study of the Scriptures and their revelation of God. They urge us to give up our superficial views of God's being. And that is all to the good. We need that.

9

I hope that I have listened to their plea. My second thesis is especially for such men and women.

To all my readers I say again: *God is worthy of being known and proclaimed for who He is, and that fact is an important part of the missionary motive and message.*

To you who have grasped that point I repeat: *those who know the most about God are the most responsible and best equipped to tell of Him.*

# 1: 'It Pleased God'

**A**

Years ago, a missionary went from the West to the East to carry his message. One day as he was preaching a listener interrupted him. 'That's a good tale,' said he, 'but I have a question. If what you say is true, why have I not heard of it before? Why did my father never hear this message, and my grandfather before him? Surely, if it were true, someone would have told my people long before now.'

The missionary was at a loss for an answer. Finally he said, 'The Lord Jesus left orders with His church to take this message everywhere. But the church has been slow in doing it. You know how people are; they do not always do what they are told.' And with that the missionary went back to his preaching. But when he came home on furlough he asked various churches, 'How would you have answered that question?' And for the most part his listeners did not know what to say. So they shuffled their feet and looked at the floor. Perhaps that is what I did the first time I heard that story.

With varying details that story has been told over and over again. The details change because the same question has been raised by people in many places. The story rings true. It is the very question we might have asked had we been in their place. I would have asked it. So would you. The gospel has been in the world for thousands of years. Why are there so many who have never heard?

Let us leave that story, however, and turn to another that concerns William Carey. Carey, you may remember, is thought of as the father of modern missions. He went out to India in 1793. There he spent the rest of his life, preaching and praying and preparing translations of the New Testament in many languages. Carey toiled in India until 1834 when his Lord called him to Himself. It is said that the printing work that Carey directed 'rendered the Bible accessible to more than three hundred million people.'

But there was little success at the outset. Instead there was unrelieved opposition, the kind of opposition the natural man always offers to the gospel. Let me give you a sample. It is taken from a talk Carey had with a Brahman in 1797. At that time Carey had not yet baptized his first convert.

The Brahman was defending the worship of idols. Carey cited Acts 14:16 and 17:30:

> God formerly 'suffered all nations to walk in their own ways,' said Carey, 'but now commandeth all men everywhere to repent.'
>
> 'Indeed,' said the native, 'I think God ought to repent for not sending the gospel sooner to us.'

This was the Brahman's direct way of saying that he did not believe Carey's message. In sharper words it is the same objection we have already seen: 'If what you say is true, why have I not heard of it before?'

Here, however, the story takes a new turn. William Carey was at no loss for words. Nor did he back down. Instead he launched a counter-attack. He assured the Brahman that God is never guilty of an injustice:

> To this I added [Carey says], suppose a kingdom had been long overrun by the enemies of its true king, and he, though possessed of sufficient power to conquer them, should yet suffer them to prevail, and establish themselves as much as they could desire, would not the valour and wisdom of that king be far more conspicuous in exterminating them, than it would have been if he had opposed them at first, and prevented their entering the country? Thus by the diffusion of gospel light, the wisdom, power, and grace of God will be more conspicuous in overcoming such deep-rooted idolatries, and in destroying all that darkness and vice which have so universally prevailed in this country, than they would have been if all had not been suffered to walk in their own ways for so many ages past.

Here is an answer we have not heard before! Let us see what it means.

In brief Carey says two things:

1) At one time it pleased God to keep back the gospel from India.

2) God had His reasons for doing so.

It was for His own glory to allow India to sink deep into corruption. His rescuing it, then, would shine more brightly in the eyes of men and angels. In that way God would display the greatness of His wisdom and power and grace.

I do not know how the Brahman received this answer. He may have scoffed at it. From the point of view of a rebel against God, neither Carey's answer nor the answer of the other missionaries would make much sense.

You and I, however, are not heathen. So we must ask a question of our own: Which of these answers is the one that ought to have been given? Which of them is true? In answering that question we can do something of great importance. We can catch the missionary vision that God intends us to pursue in these days.

**B**

Which of these answers is true and which is false? There are important differences between these two answers. Yet I doubt that the best thing to say is that one is true and the other false. The two answers look at the problem in different ways. Let me show you what I mean.

The first answer was:

> The Lord Jesus left orders with His church to take this message everywhere. But the church has been slow in doing it. You know how people are; they do not always do what they are told.

Here is a standard response to the question, 'Why have we not heard before this?'

Surely this answer is true. The command to bring the gospel to all men jumps out at us from the pages of the Bible. Yet we have been slow to do it. Even now, so late in history, it has not been fully done. One might think that the Lord had never said, 'Ye shall be witnesses unto me . . . unto the uttermost part of the earth' (Acts 1:8). Did He not say, 'Go . . . teach all nations' (Matthew 28:19)? How, then, are so many left in darkness without a ray of hope?

Jesus once asked some men, 'Why call ye me, Lord, Lord, and do not the things which I say' (Luke 6:46)? Does He ask us that also? Does He say, 'Why have you not taken My gospel to all men?' He would seem to have great reason to do so. We, for our part, would seem to be without an adequate answer. Can you think of one – an *adequate* answer? I cannot.

One might think that shame would now drive us to our task. Do the commands of our Lord mean so little to us? Are we indifferent to Him? Or, if not shame, pity on those who have not heard. Are we unconcerned at the cries of the heathen? Can we weep at television drama and sit dry-eyed before the needs of the lost?

Such questions shame us, yet I know that shame will not move us as we ought to be moved. We will need a larger motive than our own humiliation to finish the task. Even the spiritual poverty of the pagan will not do it. We must have a grander vision. And that brings us to the second answer we have seen, the answer of William Carey.

## C

Briefly again, William Carey said:

1) At one time it pleased God to keep back the gospel from India, and

2) God had His reasons for doing so.

This is a surprising answer. To some it is likely to be a shocking answer as well. Let us see if we can

15

understand it. Or, better still, let us see if we can grasp *why* Carey said this. We understand his answer well enough. We know what it means. That is why it surprises and shocks us.

To help us, let me borrow two phrases from our books of theology. The first is 'the responsibility of man'; the second is 'the sovereignty of God.' These phrases, no doubt, are not new to us. They represent two truths. They also stand for two ways of looking at history. A brief glance at each will prove helpful.

What do we mean by 'the responsibility of man?' We mean, of course, that man must answer to God for what he does. God did not make man for man to go his own way. Man was made to serve God. To that end God gave man rules by which to live. Man is responsible to do what God says. We may even go a step further, and say that man is responsible to be what God tells him to be. This is the responsibility of man.

Now this truth, the truth of man's responsibility to God, helps us to understand life. It gives us a standpoint from which to look at history. We hear of wars, for instance. We hear of economic crises. We watch our political leaders and see the results of their actions. Why do these things happen? Why is the earth filled with turmoil, and why is it a stranger to peace? Why is history the way it is? How can we make sense of this?

We can answer these questions in terms of man's responsibility. We may say: Man has not served God. Man has not lived by God's rules. Man has not done what God required him to do. Man has not been what God told him to be.

The same kind of answer can be given to the question, 'Why have so many heathen not yet heard the gospel?' Man's responsibility comes in here. So we may repeat the common answer. We may say, 'You know how people are. They do not always do what they are told.' And that answer is perfectly true, as far as it goes.

It does not, however, go far enough. Right here we may make a grave mistake. We may suppose that we have said all that can be said. If we think in this way, we reckon without God. Specifically, we reckon without the sovereignty of God.

What do we mean by the sovereignty of God? We mean that God rules in His creation. We mean that He reigns as King over all that He has made. We mean, to borrow the words of a man who himself was a king,

> God doeth according to his will in the army of heaven, and among the inhabitants of the earth: and none can stay his hand . . . (Nebuchadnezzar, speaking in Daniel 4:35).

We mean that history is 'His story.' This is the sovereignty of God.

I have had a curious experience with these words, 'the sovereignty of God.' Let me tell you about it. It seems that when I use these words in conversation they frequently draw forth the quick response, 'Oh, I believe in the sovereignty of God!' Yes, and with an exclamation mark! It happens repeatedly. Every Christian, it seems, wants to be known as a believer in the sovereignty of God. And that is all to the good.

But I find something else. I find that these same Christians do not often explain things by God's sovereignty. Some would see God's hand in what are called

17

'natural disasters.' Natural disasters would show a sovereign God at work. Others would not go so far. They would see God's sovereignty only in apparent blessings. If they receive a large sum of money they will say that God sent it. If their health suddenly improves they give the credit to God. They may even say, 'Our sovereign God sent that blessing.' And, as I have said, that is all to the good. But they hesitate to go further.

I think I understand that hesitation. I do not mean to make light of it. It is a fear, is it not, of making God the author of sin? So that, when sin is involved, they chalk up the event to man or to Satan. 'Yes,' they say, 'God rules. God is sovereign. We believe all that. But we don't want to charge God with the results of sin. Sin is man's responsibility, not God's!' Or, 'Satan was at work here. Let's not speak of God!'

We may put their objection in theological terms. They are saying to us: 'Let us not replace human responsibility by the sovereignty of God.' And when they say that, we must listen to them. But we must also correct them. We must start by rejecting their choice. We must say firmly: 'It is not human responsibility *or* God's sovereignty. It is not one or the other. It is human responsibility *and* God's sovereignty. Let us not replace the sovereignty of God by human responsibility.'

Let me show you why this is so. If God rules only in those places or events where no sin is involved, God does not rule on this earth. If sin can thwart God, His sovereignty is a name and not a fact. He may rule on Mars or Saturn. But He does not rule here. We can easily show that this is so.

18

The fact is that sin is involved in everything that man does. Since the fall of man this has been so. To begin with, all that natural men do is sinful. Their carnal minds are 'not subject to the law of God, neither indeed can be. So then they that are in the flesh cannot please God' (Romans 8:7, 8). This is God's estimate of all natural men.

Yet these are the men who 'run' the world. With few exceptions, they are the kings, the presidents, the prime ministers, and the economists. And they are the prophets and priests of earth's billions.

What place then is left for God? None at all, if God does not rule where sin is present. Better to give up the phrase, 'the sovereignty of God', than to empty it of its content. If the kernel of truth is gone, we need not keep the husk of empty words.

Nor is that all. If God does not rule where sin exists then He does not rule even in the hearts of Christians. 'For there is no man that sinneth not' (2 Chronicles 6:36). And 'if we say that we have no sin, we deceive ourselves, and the truth is not in us' (1 John 1:8). Here also, in the heart of the Christian, sin will have dethroned God.

To meet this problem some would limit God's sovereignty to the close of history. They say, 'God will pull all the pieces together some day. He will make it all come out right at last.' No doubt He will! Still, if this is all that His sovereignty means, His hands are effectually tied right now.

But can we believe this? Surely not! We cannot believe it and we dare not believe it. All Scripture is against it. God reigns. That is the stance of the Word of God. Did not our Lord Jesus say, 'All power is given

19

unto me in heaven and in earth' (Matthew 28:18)? Has He abdicated His throne? No! and no power in heaven or in earth can pull it down around Him!

I have said that human responsibility gives us a standpoint from which to look at history. And so it does. But so also does God's sovereignty. We hear of wars and economic crises. We watch our political leaders and see the results of their actions. Why do these things happen? Why is history the way it is? We have answered these questions from the standpoint of man's responsibility. And our answers are true. Men have failed to serve God. Man has not done what God has told him to do.

But these answers, while true, are not complete. There is another answer. There is another standpoint from which to view our world – the standpoint of God's sovereignty.

And what then? What if God reigns? We dare not deny man's responsibility. We cannot insist that Christians have done all that they ought to have done. And we need not pretend that we have solved the problem of how God can rule in the midst of sin without defiling Himself. God knows the answer to that. I do not.

Since God reigns, however, there is something we must say. We must say it as clearly as we say that man has failed. We must say, with William Carey:

1) *It pleased God . . .* , and

2) *God has His reasons.*

There is an instinct in Carey's answer, the instinct to resort to God. How we need that! To be sure, we must hold fast to our responsibility. Let us not lose sight of that! But above all else we must pray for this:

to learn to speak and think and feel in these terms. It pleased God! God had His reasons! In the final analysis – God!

21

## 2: *Renouncing the Utilitarian God*

This book is about missions, but we must not move too fast. Before a man is a missionary he must be a Christian; the roots of the missionary's attitudes lie in the Christian. We have a proverb, 'the child is the father of the man'. So also the Christian is the father of the missionary. If, then, the missionary ought to be God-centred, it will be because the Christian must be God-centred. So we raise a question. What is there in the Christian life that prepares us for God-centredness? What will lead us to say, 'In the final analysis – God!'?

### A

I want you to think – and not in a vague, general way – about what happens to a man when he becomes a Christian. I have in view one specific description of what then happens. It is not my description. It is that of the apostle Paul. Paul wrote to the Christians at Corinth and described the beginning of the Christian life. He spoke of it as the coming of 'the light of the knowledge of the glory of God' (2 Corinthians 4:6).

Paul meant this: when a man becomes a Christian he sees God in a new way. He sees God's glory. There is a splendour, a magnificence, a majesty about God that he did not see before. The Christian is a new man, and he has a new awareness of God. That is Paul's position.

You may remember your new vision of God when you became a Christian. But it is not vital that you remember it. The evidence that you had a new, richer view of God will be the same whether you can recall it or not. The evidence is this. You became a worshipper of God. God was seeking worshippers, and He laid hold on you. If we had to give a name to Christians, we might call them 'true worshippers of the true God.' That is not all that a Christian is, but that is basic. A Christian is a worshipper of God. If you are not a worshipper of God, you are not a Christian.

Now here comes the important point. *Worship is a response to greatness.* A man does not become a worshipper merely by saying, 'Now I shall become a worshipper.' That is impossible. That cannot be done. A man becomes a worshipper when he sees something great that calls forth his admiration or his worship. That is the only way worshippers are made. Worship answers to greatness. In the words of the Puritan, Thomas Watson, 'We glorify God, when we are God-admirers.'

Of course, we can make imitation worshippers. We can teach men to say the right things and to sing the right songs. And we can call what they do 'worship'. Yes, we can do all that and we can deceive ourselves and deceive them into thinking that they are worshipping God. But we cannot make them true worshippers. Only God can do that. And He does it by throwing light on His own character, His own person. When a man sees that light he becomes a worshipper. Worship is man's response to perceived greatness.

23

It is very important that we understand this. We hold, for example, meetings that we call 'worship services'. Now what are these? Are they meetings where we become worshippers? No, not at all. If we are not worshippers when we come to the meetings we shall not be worshippers in the meetings. There is only one exception to this rule. If God makes us Christians – if we are born again – while we are in the meeting, then we shall become worshippers. But that is the only exception. Otherwise coming to the service will not make us worshippers at all.

So then, when a man becomes a Christian he sees God in a new way. He comes to the 'knowledge of the glory of God.' He sees a splendour, a magnificence about God that he did not see before. The new-born Christian finds that he has begun to 'know the only true God, and Jesus Christ whom He has sent.' And he worships the Almighty.

It would be possible, of course, to overstate this. We must not think of the new Christian in the wrong way. We must not think of him as being born full-grown. God is not nearly so splendid to the new Christian as He will be later. The Christian has much to learn. We must not deny that. Yet this remains true: the new Christian has a new vision of God. And that vision is majestic, glorious.

Let us go a step further. Once a man is a Christian, what then? Here again Paul will help us. If we ask him what his own way of life is, he is ready with an answer:

> I count all things but loss for the excellency of the knowledge of Christ Jesus my Lord (Philippians 3:8).

Nothing can be compared with knowing Christ. Why

does Paul say 'Christ' here rather than 'God'? Has Christ come to compete with God for Paul's affection? Not at all! In Christ God is best revealed. Paul first saw the glory of God 'in the face of Jesus Christ'. It is in that same face – that is, in that same person – that Paul expects to find further glimpses of God's glory. Paul seeks to know Christ so that he may better know God.

The Christian life, then, is born in the knowledge of God. It grows as it increases in the knowledge of God. Maturity is, in large part, finding the answers to this question: What is God like?

And when we come to the end of our days, what then? Here also the Bible leaves us in no doubt. The future will bring us a fresh view of what God is like, and together with all other true Christians, we shall celebrate that new disclosure.

Paul tells us about that further knowledge of God:

> Now we see through a glass, darkly; but then face to face: now I know in part; but then shall I know even as also I am known (1 Corinthians 13:12).

To know as I am known will be to know God in a way that I cannot know Him here. Or, as John puts it, 'We shall see him [the Lord Jesus] as he is' (1 John 3:2).

We must not think of this fuller knowledge of God as given to us to satisfy our curiosity. No doubt it will do that; but it will do much more. It will excite us to praise God as we have never yet done.

You may feel that coming excitement in words from the Book of Revelation:

> And every creature which is in heaven, and on the earth, and under the earth, and such as are in the sea, and

25

all that are in them, heard I saying, Blessing, and honour, and glory, and power, be unto him that sitteth upon the throne, and unto the Lamb for ever and ever (5:13).

Among these creatures are men. Why do they say such things? Not because they are programmed to do so! Rather they are overwhelmed by the knowledge of God. God is worthy of being known for who He is – that is their conviction – and they glory in Him.

This is not a tedious task to them. Not at all! It is a work worthy of those who have been made 'kings and priests to God' (5:10).

## B

But let us come back from heaven to our own world. I have said three things about the Christian life.

1) It is born in the knowledge of God.

2) It matures as it grows in the knowledge of God.

3) Its goal is the fullest vision of God's glory and greatness. Here, in other words, is the meaning of life.

The man who does not know God is dead. The man who knows God, and is coming to know Him better, is powerfully alive. As we have already repeated, Jesus said to His Father,

> This is life eternal, that they might know thee, the only true God, and Jesus Christ, whom thou hast sent (John 17:3).

Men must know God. That is the one thing they must do. And this can mean nothing less than that God is eminently worthy to be known in all the length and breadth and height and depth of His character. The

Christian is a God-explorer. The Christian vision is the vision of God.

The missionary vision is the vision of God also. It is not something different from the Christian vision. It is the same vision being shared rather than merely enjoyed. It is the same vision being shared with men who have no natural taste for it, in the hope that God will create that taste so that they too will become 'God-admirers'. Sharing the vision of God – that is the work of missions.

In this sense – the deepest and truest sense – we are all missionaries. You must not suppose, and I must not imply, that the impulses and inspirations that move our missionaries are at all different from the motives that ought to move every Christian. That must be the furthest thing from our minds. Perhaps we have no thought of going abroad. It may not be the thing for us to do. But that will make no difference. We too must have the highest and best inducements for what we do. And they will turn out to be the same motives that the missionary ought to have, no more, and no less.

But we have come to use the word 'missionary' for one who leaves his culture, if not his country, to serve Christ. That is the way I will use the word also. The principles, however, will apply to us all.

C

What then is the missionary to do? The Psalmist answers, 'Declare his glory among the nations!' (Psalm 96:3). Here is a work worthy of the noblest workman. But it is liable to be like one of those grand ideas that sometimes take hold of us, only to be dismissed when

27

the telephone rings or the milkman comes and we are brought back to what we like to call 'the real world.'

'Yes,' someone says, 'that's it. We need to proclaim the glory of God. No doubt about it! But I need to know how to do that in practical terms. Can you help me?'

Well, I have no 'how-to' programme. If someone wants a method that he can use later this week I cannot help him. But there is another way to look at this problem. You can *think* in different terms. And that is what I believe you ought to do. You need to think, not of an instant programme, but of increasing your own knowledge of God to the point where speaking of His glory becomes a part of you. Each Christian, missionary or not, ought to do this. Remember that those who sing around God's throne are not programmed to do so. It is meat and drink to them to declare the glory of God.

But how are we to start? One answer is to come to grips with the times in which we live. We live in the age of 'the utilitarian god' (the phrase is A. W. Tozer's), the god who can be used for our own ends. Suppose we want happiness and success. How shall we get them? This god is waiting in the wings to give them to us. Let us find just the right formula for approaching him and we may have our heart's desire!

Here is a god worth knowing for what he does, or, more specifically, for what he gives. There is no need to look behind this god's gifts. Men do not care particularly what he is like, any more than they care to know the character of the clerk that they speak to on their telephone. If he can do the errand that needs to be done, that is all they ask. His personal traits are his own business. Let him be what he pleases.

Now we must renounce this god once and for all. I do not mean, of course, that any true Christian has followed 'the utilitarian god'. A Christian could not possibly do that. For one thing, there is nothing in such a god to inspire worship. The god-who-serves-ME requires flattery, not worship. A Christian, as we have seen, is a worshipper of God. If he is not that, he is not a Christian. No, the Christian does not follow 'the utilitarian god'.

But there is another side to this. Is it possible that the Christian may colour his own view of the true God by what he hears of 'the utilitarian god?' You and I must look that question in the face. And when we do, we shall find, I fear, that this has happened to many among us. Perhaps it has happened to you and me. That is why we must renounce the god-who-serves-ME for ever.

Take, for instance, the matter of success. The 'utilitarian god' promises success to his followers. Do we suppose that, if we serve the true God with zeal and devotion, we may count on Him to make us successful? I live in a success-centred society, a success-oriented culture. Shall I expect God to take note of that and to reward my service with results that will satisfy me, that will make me feel good about what I have done? In other words, do I expect God to be my servant to that extent?

Well, in all probability God will disappoint me. He may plan to teach me that *faithfulness* is success, whether that agrees with the spirit of modern society or not. God may determine to cure me of my worldliness. For, after all, worldliness is adopting the attitudes of the world around me, no more and no less.

Or let us take the matter of health. Our culture is not only success-oriented, it is also youth-centred. But youth is the time of vigour, of health. How does that affect me? I fear it makes me crave health excessively. Do not misunderstand me. I am aware that good health is a great boon. I do not want to minimize it. I know how easy it is for me – I am in good health – to write and speak glibly. But there is a greater blessing than health, as every Christian knows. That is to be in the will of God. And however much I want to keep my vigour, I must learn to say of health as of all else, 'Thy will be done.'

We must not allow the TV, when its screen is swollen with robust young bodies, to shape our attitudes for us. If God gives us health let us be adoringly grateful. But we must not 'use' God for health or anything else. If there is any *using* to be done, far better that He should do it! Of this we may be sure: there is infinite wisdom behind any use He may make of us.

This is the first step, then: to renounce 'the utilitarian god'. I may indeed pray for both success and health. I certainly want both, along with many other things. For anything it is right to want, it is right to pray. And God has told us that often we have not because we ask not. But that is not all He has told us. He has told us to pray, 'Thy will be done in earth, as it is in heaven' (Matthew 6:10). And if we have ever prayed that prayer and meant it – even once – we have ourselves shut the door on thousands of things for which we might foolishly ask.

The first step, the step of renunciation, is easy to

explain. That does not mean that it is easy to do. But it does mean that we need not take more time discussing it. The second step, the positive step, is quite different. It will require most of the rest of the book. What I mean to do is to survey the attributes of God. I do not mean to be exhaustive. I will not speak of them all. Instead I want to make a selection, and with each of them to talk to you about its bearing on world missions. I hope you will want to stay with me.

# 3: *God, Self-sufficient*

It seems best to start with *the self-sufficiency of God*. Perhaps the phrase is not a familiar one. We do not often speak of God's self-sufficiency, but that is our loss. Right here, we may find, is the root of much shallow thinking about God.

**A**

God's self-sufficiency means that there is nothing that God needs. Or, we might say that God has no other need than to please Himself.

Even if we were not Christians we might readily believe this. We might hold that God launched the universe into space and then went on His way, much as a boy idly blows his hundredth soap bubble and cares nothing for its fate. In fact, this seems to be the view of many around us. Ask them if they believe in God and they answer 'Yes'. Ask them if God enters into relations with men and they say, 'No'. God exists, but He has gone His way, they know not where.

It is this whole question of relationships, you see, that raises the question of God's self-sufficiency acutely. If God is more than Creator, if He is Lawgiver and Judge and Saviour – and He is all of these – then we have a problem. We may put it in the form of a question. What need does God fulfil in entering into these relations? Why did He not enjoy alone the riches of His own Being for ever? And this question has no answer that I know of, beyond saying that it pleased Him so to act.

Yet the Bible is clear about this. Ignorant worship, Paul told the men of Athens, is worship prompted by the idea that God needs something from us. That is its mistake. God, he said, is not 'worshipped with men's hands, as though he needed anything' (Acts 17:25). The world needs God. That is where the need lies. God does not need the world.

Paul has been criticized for his message at Athens. For instance:

> There the apostle had met the philosophers on their own ground ... And his speech was triumphant as oratory, as logic, and as a specimen of philosophic thought; but in its bearing on conversion it was unsuccessful. His work at Athens was a failure ...

The thought is that Paul failed to preach Christ. Had he done so, he would have been successful. Poor Paul!

But Paul was wiser than his critics. It was not enough to Paul to speak of *God* and *Christ*. The words must be given content. And Paul knew what many today forget, that the natural man has a false view of God. To say that 'God so loved the world' is to convey nothing true unless men have some idea of the true God. To go on to speak of God's Son is to invite men to put Christ on the same degraded level as their notion of God. But that will not do. And Paul knew it. What we have here is not 'a specimen of philosophic thought'. What we have is a sample of Christian preaching to Gentiles, cut

33

short perhaps by the scorn of the crowd. 'God needs nothing' is not mere philosophy. It is Christian doctrine as well.

We have not gone the full way, however, until we have made this as personal as possible. 'God needs nothing' means that God does not need *me*. I may not like that fact, but there it is. It puts me in my place. God does not need me and He does not need you.

Once, when I was a boy, I heard a man say, 'I like coloured people – in their place.' His emphasis was on those last three words, 'in their place.' But what he meant was all wrong. When he used those words – they were common words in those days – he meant that he liked to see black people in the place white folks picked out for them. Of course he did! We all like everybody when they are willing to go where we want them to go, and stay in the place where we want them to stay.

But if he had meant those words in another way he would have been correct. God has the right to put us in our place: all of us, of whatever colour. And He has done so. He has done it be telling us that He does not need us. Jesus taught us to say, 'We are unprofitable servants' (Luke 17:10). The self-sufficiency of God is not only true in itself, it is immensely practical. It helps us to grasp the immeasurable gulf between God and ourselves. We can add nothing to God. He needs nothing to be added.

God's self-sufficiency also means that I cannot bargain with God. That was Paul's point with the Athenians. 'You must give up the idea,' he was saying, 'that you can barter so much worship for so much of God's good will.' I must cease to think of

God in a commercial way. On His part, He needs nothing. On my part, I have nothing to give. Trade on this basis is unthinkable. I am God's debtor, but He can never be mine.

Let us see how God's self-sufficiency bears on missions. I want to come to this subject by quoting A. W. Tozer. Tozer strikes me, as he has many others, as a 20th-century prophet. Here are his words.

> We commonly represent [God] as a busy, eager, somewhat frustrated Father hurrying about seeking help to carry out His benevolent plan to bring peace and salvation to the world . . .
>
> Too many missionary appeals are based upon this fancied frustration of Almighty God. An effective speaker can easily excite pity in his hearers, not only for the heathen but for the God who has tried so hard and so long to save them and has failed for want of support. I fear that thousands of young persons enter Christian service from no higher motive than to help deliver God from the embarrassing situation His love has gotten Him into and his limited abilities seem unable to get Him out of. Add to this a certain degree of commendable idealism and a fair amount of compassion for the underprivileged and you have the true drive behind much Christian activity today.

These are remarkable words. Let us see why.

First, they are remarkable because of the position of the man who wrote them. They are not the words of a man content to sit and watch the world wend its way to hell. Far from it! A. W. Tozer was the editor of the *Alliance Witness*, a periodical devoted to the spread of the gospel. The large band of missionaries of the Christian and Missionary Alliance were often fed and moved by the pen of this man. Tozer was a missionary at heart.

But Tozer's zeal for missions did not blind him. He saw that more was at stake in our preaching than we commonly realize. God's name, God's honour, and God's character are at stake. We dare not misrepresent Him. If we ignore these things we ignore God Himself. What right have we then to call ourselves His servants?

Let us take a closer look at Tozer's indictment. The thing we must see is the connection, the inseparable connection, between our view of God and our attitude toward missions. Is God frustrated? Are His hands tied? Does He require something not found in Himself to carry out His plans? How shall we answer these questions?

Tozer's point is clear. The way we answer these questions has everything to do with the kind of missionaries we shall be. Yet we have given careless answers to these questions in the past. Our zeal for the work has carried us away. In fact, it has led us to pervert the character of God!

There is double tragedy here. This touches both motive and message. If our motive is pity for God it is a false motive. We are those who need pity! Nothing is more tragic than an impoverished view of God. A Christian lives by faith. He does not live by sight. But faith is not nourished by a god who needs our pity. Quite the opposite! Try as we may, we cannot wholly trust a god who needs our sympathy.

And what of our message? That, too, is bound to go wrong. We may preach about a greater God than He in whom, actually, we believe. That is, we may parrot the right words. But I doubt that we can convey the truth to others. It will be a case of our actions speaking so loudly that men will not hear what we say with our lips. Here, in list form, is the way things may turn out if our ideas of God are not as lofty as they ought to be.

1) We will preach the God of the Bible, using the right words.

2) Men will hear our words.

3) They will also see our lack of faith.

4) They will either:

    a. accept our message and have the same reservations about the greatness of God that we have, or

    b. they will write us off as hypocrites and reject what we say.

If they receive our message, we may rejoice. But if we are wise we will do something else also. We will grieve that another generation and another culture has been taught from the outset to think unworthy thoughts of God.

But even 'right words' are too much to hope for. Experience shows that we will not hang on to right words about God. Why should we? Our ideas will affect our words. That is the way the mind usually works. I live in a large city in the United States. I can test the quality of our words quite simply, without leaving my home. All I need to do is to turn on my radio.

The Christian stations in and around my city broadcast words about God day and night. Too often they are unworthy words – more times than I care to count. I am not speaking here of those speakers who could be called false prophets. We have an ample supply of those also. No, I am speaking of those who are highly respected in Christian circles.

37

Let me cite a case. Yesterday I heard a popular radio speaker, a good man, call faith 'an illogical process'. He did not say it in passing. It was part of a definition of faith that he used more than once. I think I know what he meant. He meant that faith in Christ does not make sense to the natural man. And, of course, he was right. Faith is foolishness to the natural man, because his mind is darkened. His reason is perverted. I know what he meant – at least I hope I know! – after years of study. But what hope was there that the unconverted man would understand? Or the new Christian? Very little.

Look what is implied if faith is 'an illogical process'. It means that faith is against reason. But it is God who demands faith. Is God against reason? Does He not address our reason all through His Word? Does He not say, 'Come now, and let us reason together . . .' (Isaiah 1:18)?

Let us look at this more closely. If God asks us to reason with Him, what shall we do? Shall we obey? That would be the *logical* thing to do. But if logic is to be left out of the picture, then what? Why, then, we do not know what to do. Then we may say, 'No!' It is no good to remind us that it is God speaking, for we may abandon our logic when we deal with God! In fact, we must do so if faith is an illogical process.

Now if this seems like utter nonsense – and it is nonsense of the worst kind – look what it says about God. On this view, God commands nonsense. I leave you to imagine what kind of a god commands nonsense. It will not be the God of the Bible. The God of the Bible may call on us to do what we cannot understand. But it will not be because what He requires is illogical.

It will be because our little minds cannot grasp His reasons. It will be because He knows best, not because He cares nothing about logic and understanding. It will not be because God Himself is confused.

Now I know that no Christian will say that God is confused. Such a thought is blasphemous. Nevertheless there is the risk that vague notions about God will be implanted in the mind by this confusion. And they will not be lofty notions. When they are added to other false ideas about God the result will be disaster. Faith must feed on God as He is, if it is to be true faith. Faith, to be robust, must have worthy thoughts of God.

The case I have cited is a case in which the speaker's thoughts were really more right than his words. Something far worse happens when both words and thoughts are debased. We can see this in Tozer's statement. God, Tozer tells us, is made to appear frustrated by much modern preaching. This happens in missionary appeals. The idea is left that God *needs* our help. We are not told that He graciously offers us the opportunity to take part in the great missionary enterprise. No, things have gone much beyond that; in fact, they have gotten out of hand. There may have been a time when God could have made such an offer, but that time is long past. Things are now desperate. A great deal that should have been done for God's cause has not been done. And God is rushing around to make up for lost time. His love has worked Him into a corner, and He needs us to get Him out of it.

How do we correct this kind of thinking? We must correct it by the Word of God. The description of God in the last paragraph is ridiculous. It is ridiculous because it is *wrong*. There is such a thing as truth about God. That truth is in God's Word, the Bible. It will not do for us to imagine what God is like. We dare not conjecture about His supposed needs. It is our imaginations and our conjectures and our suppositions that betray us. What we need is fact. And the fact, in this case, is that God is self-sufficient. He is *never* frustrated. He is not like we are. Sometimes we are calm. But calm is not native to us fallen men. We know that frustration of one sort or another is just around the corner. We are not self-sufficient. We are not God.

But if we are not God, we may nevertheless know God. If we know the God of the Bible we know the God who is eminently worthy of being known. If we are humbled, He is exalted. And if God helps us we may yet learn to rejoice in His self-sufficiency. If God brings us out of our stupor we may hear such words as the following with jubilation:

> [God is not] worshipped with men's hands, as though he needed any thing, seeing he giveth to all life, and breath, and all things . . . (Acts 17:25),

and this:

> Where wast thou when I laid the foundations of the earth? (Job 38:4),

and this:

> If I were hungry, I would not tell thee: for the world is mine, and the fulness thereof (Psalm 50:12),

and this:

> My word . . . shall not return unto me void, but it shall

accomplish that which I please, and it shall prosper in the thing whereto I sent it (Isaiah 55:11),

and this above all:

I will build my church! (Matthew 16:18).

Here is the God worthy to be known and to be proclaimed for who He is!

# 4: *God's Sovereign Power*

Some pages back I told you a story about William Carey. From it I gave you a bare-bones outline of what Carey said to a native listener. Do you remember how Carey explained why much of India had not earlier heard the gospel? Carey said:

1) It pleased God . . . , and
2) God has His reasons

I do not know what the Brahman made of this. He probably scoffed. But that was Carey's answer, right or wrong. And I think it was right, because it is biblical.

Looking more closely at this outline we see that it implies two things about God. Let me put them down next to the outline.

1) It pleased God.     God is sovereign.
2) God has His reasons     God is wise.

I have already said a few things about God's sovereignty. In this chapter I must say much more.

### A

I would like us to look at God's sovereignty from two angles. Let me call the one 'the sovereignty of God's power.' The other I will call 'the sovereignty of

God's grace.' But first I must say a word about these divisions.

Anyone who thinks about it will realize that God's person cannot be divided up as neatly as this implies. You cannot do that with any person. You cannot separate a man's character into neat compartments. You can talk about his loves and his hatreds, his envy and his desire, his wisdom and his power, but when you have finished you are left with but one person looked at in many ways.

This is even more true of God. In God there are no inner contradictions. God is one harmonious whole. His sovereignty and His justice and His wisdom are, after all, just Himself looked at from different sides. That is why we cannot fix the number of God's attributes. It depends on how you look at Him. And so we might think of God's sovereignty in six ways, or in ten ways, instead of two. But these two will do for now. What we are after is to know God, that we may worship Him. The divisions we make are just a way to get to that goal.

William Carey was talking to the Brahman about the sovereignty of God's power. It was in God's hand to send the gospel or not to send it. God did what He pleased. He exercised His power. First, He withheld the gospel, then He gave it.

God's sovereignty means that God does as He pleases. What freedom God has! He is not like I am. In my worst moments I seek to do as I please, but I cannot carry it off. I have neither the power nor the right to assert that kind of freedom. But God has! God has never yet put forth His power without a perfect right to do so. In God these three things meet: pleasure,

43

power, and right. God has the authority and the might to do as He pleases.

One thing that pleases God is to give commands. He makes men and He tells them what to do. God made Adam. Then He told Adam to care for the garden and to look after the trees. Finally He told Adam to help himself to the fruit of all the trees but one. God's commands were positive ('do this!') and negative ('do not do that!'). It pleased God to command His creature, and it pleased Adam to obey. God was King and Adam was God's servant.

To this point in the story it is easy to trace God's lordship. Adam did what God told him to do, and he did it cheerfully. All Christians, I think, can see the sovereignty of God at work here. But then something happened. Man sinned. It takes just two words to say it – 'man sinned' – but Christians are agreed that you cannot measure the import of what happened by the few words it takes to describe it. Enormous changes took place. We could list these changes at some length, but at this point only one of them requires comment.

Adam made a frontal attack on the sovereignty of God. In effect, Adam said: 'You have been King till now. But now I shall be King. Now I will pursue my own purposes. Your lordship, God, is over.' Fallen man sets himself up in competition to the God he sinned against. This is what sin does. It seeks to dethrone God. Sin snatches at His crown. Sin says: 'Away with the sovereignty of God!'

But we must slow down. We must not move too fast. The question is: Does sin succeed? Are God's purposes thwarted by sin? And the answer to that question is remarkable. It is not at all what we might

44

have expected. The answer is this: Adam the sinner furthered the purposes of God to the same degree as Adam the righteous. He did not aim to do so, but that is what Adam did.

Before I seek to prove this from Scripture, let us try to understand what it means. Please note what I did *not* say. I did not say that Adam furthered the purposes of God *in the same way* as Adam the righteous. Not at all! Adam the righteous sought to please God and to serve God as his Lord. Adam the sinner did the opposite. His way was wholly different. The new way was the reverse of the old – what is sometimes called 'an 180° turn.' No one could confuse Adam's new intention with his old one.

But Adam's intention is not the whole story. What Adam aimed to do and what Adam actually managed to do are not the same. In a different way, *but in the same degree*, Adam carried forward the purpose of God. Adam's act was sinful because he did not aim to please God. His motive was wrong, and God judged him for it. But God meant to use even that evil to advance His own glory.

To see this more clearly, let us compare it with the story of the sin of Joseph's brothers, given later in Genesis. Joseph's brothers hated him. For that reason Joseph was a marked young man. Time was on the brother's side. Sooner or later their chance to dispose of him would come. And they would do it with relish.

The day finally came. Midianite slave traders passed near the spot where the brothers were tending their flocks, and his brothers sold Joseph into slavery. The deal netted them twenty pieces of silver, and they

45

washed their hands of Joseph for ever. Or so they thought.

In fact, their act proved to be only the beginning of the story. When famine later struck Canaan, the brothers were forced to go down into Egypt to buy grain. And what did they find? They found Joseph – not now a slave, but the virtual ruler of Egypt – and they were at his mercy.

The story has a happy end, but only because Joseph understood the ways of God. Joseph saw more in the events of his life than the brothers' hatred. Later, when they pleaded for forgiveness, we read:

> Joseph wept when they spake unto him. And his brethren also went and fell down before his face; and they said, Behold, we be thy servants.
>
> And Joseph said unto them, Fear not: for am I in the place of God? But as for you, ye thought evil against me; but God meant it unto good, to bring to pass, as it is this day, to save much people alive (Genesis 50:17–19).

Now what has Joseph done here? He has laid his finger, has he not, on two sets of intentions, where his brothers saw but one? They intended to be done with him. And, of course, that was their sin – a sin for which they must answer. But Joseph sees more. He sees the aim of God. Israel had to find its way to Egypt, so God sent Joseph ahead to prepare a place for them. When the brothers sold Joseph they cared nothing for the purpose of God. Nevertheless, they brought it about. The sin was theirs, but the act was God's. In this, as in all else, God was King and they were His unwitting servants. The sovereignty of God held against the sinful aim of man. They, like Adam, defied God . . . and they, like Adam, carried out His purpose!

The supreme example of this sort of thing is found in the death of Christ. Suppose we ask the question, 'What was the foulest crime this earth has ever known?' What answer can we give? Surely it was the crucifixion of Jesus Christ!

But wait; let us ask another question. 'What is the foremost source of blessing?' The answer is the same. There can be no other – the crucifixion of Jesus Christ! It was the wickedest deed that men could do. See it in all its blackness! Take not a jot of its viciousness away! Viler crime than ever Adam dreamed! All that, and infinitely more!

But when you have said your worst and when you have decried the corruption of those killers' hearts, remember this. The murder of Jesus was the purpose of God. 'It pleased the Lord to bruise him' (Isaiah 53:10). God was Lord at the cross as well as at the empty tomb. Ever and always . . . God is King!

**B**

I have been talking about the sovereignty of God's power. God is free to do as He pleases, and that is what happens. Sin cannot dethrone God. That is what sin aims to do, but it misses its mark. Sin brings guilt to a man, but it does not bring him one ounce of sovereignty. God rules even when men imagine they are defying Him. The Psalmist knew this truth. Listen to him.

The kings of the earth set themselves, and the rulers

> take counsel together, against the Lord, and against His anointed . . .

And how does God react?

> He that sitteth in the heavens shall laugh: the Lord shall have them in derision (Psalm 2:2, 4).

Heaven makes merry over the conceit of the proud. God will be God, let them do what they may. God will be God, after they are forgotten.

But let us go on. I want to turn next to the sovereignty of God's grace. I mean by that phrase simply this: God dispenses His favours, the favours that have to do with salvation, as He pleases. He does not give up His lordship to anyone at any time. God remains King, even in bestowing His grace. Here are His terms:

> I will have mercy on whom I will have mercy, and I will have compassion on whom I will have compassion . . .

What conclusion must we come to, then? Paul draws it for us:

> So then it is not of him that willeth, nor of him that runneth, but of God that sheweth mercy (Romans 9:15, 16).

Man's will and man's performance do not bring salvation. Salvation is absolutely of God.

This is sometimes thought to be a hard saying. I once thought so myself. In this matter, at least, I did not want God to be God. But I was very foolish. I see now that if I had had my way, no man would have been saved. Not that that was my intention – far from it! I supposed that if men were given their way, many would turn to Christ. But I no longer think so. I have bowed to Scripture. It says,

> There is none that understandeth; there is none that seeketh after God . . . there is none that doeth good, no not one (Romans 3:11, 12).

Such men as these – and apart from God's work there is no other kind – will never turn in repentance and faith to God. Their wills are set against God. God must rescue them from themselves. He must change their bias. Otherwise they will be cast away from Him for ever.

### C

Let us try to apply these truths to missions. We have looked at the sovereignty of God in power and in grace. What effect will these great truths have on us? How do they bear on the missionary?

To begin with, here is bedrock on which the missionary can stand. We have heard David Livingstone quoted, saying, 'We are immortal until God is done with us.' How could he rightfully say such a thing? Was it mere bravado? Was he whistling in the dark? How can we be sure?

The answer lies in the sovereignty of God's power. We might call it whistling in the daylight of God's revelation. Listen to the Lord Jesus Christ on this subject.

> Are not two sparrows sold for a farthing? and one of them shall not fall on the ground without your Father . . . Fear ye not, therefore, ye are of more value than many sparrows (Matthew 10:29, 31).

Here Jesus makes the death of a sparrow a parable to us. Let us see what He means.

When Jesus tells us that sparrows do not die 'without your Father,' we want to ask a question. We want to say, 'Without your Father's *what?*' This is the key to the sentence. I am afraid that a good deal of nonsense has been spoken in answer to this question. Jesus does *not* mean that sparrows do not die without God's sympathy, for example. That is not His point at all. Yet I am sure I have heard people speak of the Father's shedding a tear in this connection. Perhaps you have heard the same thing.

I do not want to deny that God sympathizes with His creation. But that is hardly the point here. We are told to 'fear not,' but sympathy alone will not remove our fears. The point of our Lord's saying lies elsewhere. He knows that powerless sympathy will not meet the needs of His people as He thrusts them forth into the world. The missionary enjoys the sympathy, the good will, of God, unfallen angels, and of fellow believers. He values that; he does not despise it. But he needs much more than sympathy.

Jesus is telling us that no sparrow dies unless the Lord wills it. His will sustains the sparrow's life. He wills its life, and He wills its death. The point is this: God's will and power determine the life-span of a sparrow. But to the Christian I can say, This God is *your Father*. That is what you must grasp. To the sparrow God is Creator. To you, Christian, God is more. To you, God is Father.

God is a Father to every believer; to those in the hardest places as well as to those in the easy. All the richest blessings that the term 'Father' ought to suggest are poured out on every follower of Jesus Christ. That will be true of him whether he is in Manhattan or Mali, Edinburgh or Ethiopia. Everywhere and always . . . God is King on behalf of His children. Such is the sovereignty of God's power.

And what shall we say of the sovereignty of God's grace? In my judgment there could be no greater encouragement to missionary work. 'For when we were yet without strength,' Paul tells us, 'Christ died for the ungodly' (Romans 5:6). Shall we look for success to men without strength – without strength of moral character, without strength of will? If we do, we shall look in vain, for we lean on a broken reed.

But what if we look to God for our success? And what if God has 'a great multitude, which no man could number' in His eye and on His heart? Why then, we ought to take courage. Who knows what God may do? The missionary is not alone. He is accompanied by the God who has determined to have a people for Himself. And God has made up His mind to take them from 'all nations, and kindreds, and tongues' (Revelation 7:9). Here is the missionary's hope. It is not in himself. It is in God.

Finally, let us leave the matter of the Christian's safety and success behind. Not that they are unimportant! But we are on the track of a truth that transcends them. That truth is the glory of God.

In this chapter we have seen the greatness of God's sovereignty. We have hardly touched the subject, yet we have seen enough to serve our purpose. Our purpose is to know God. And in His sovereignty, as in all else about God, we have again been given our lesson. This God, who is King, is worthy to be known

51

and to be proclaimed for who He is. The missionary who proclaims this God cannot fail. If his message extols the sovereign God, it will be significant even supposing it is never the means of winning one soul. The message will not be lost. It cannot be lost. It will remain as something precious. Before men and angels – yes, and before the demons of hell – it will be praise to God! 'For we are unto God a sweet savour of Christ, in them that are saved, and in them that perish' (2 Corinthians 2:15).

# 5: *God, Fully Wise*

We come next to the subjects of the wisdom and knowledge of God. These two are closely related, so I will treat them in the same chapter. First then – the knowledge of God. Here I mean, of course, not our knowledge of God, but His knowledge of us and of all things.

## A

The theme of God's knowledge can be summed up in one phrase: God knows everything! I cannot improve on that and I will not try to do so. The statement, 'God knows everything,' is succinct and clear. My aim here is quite modest. What I hope to do, beyond reminding you that God knows all, is to give you some examples of His knowledge. What we need, it seems to me, is to be reminded about what 'everything' includes. That can be mind-expanding.

Let us consider the physical world first. God knows everything about it. Perhaps you can get some feeling for what that means if you think of the atoms of which this world is made. God knows, right now, the position of each of those atoms. And that is not all. God knows precisely where each of them was a second ago, and two seconds ago, and . . . well, I am sure you get the idea. We might project it into the future, as well. All of that, you see, is included in knowing 'everything' about the physical world.

We find the same thing if we look at the world of ungodly men. What secrets like hidden in those hearts? What purposes? God knows perfectly . . . exhaustively. Here is a felon who has devised a plan so intricate that the keenest human mind shall not find it out. Yet it lies vividly open before the mind of God. And so does its author, in all the ins-and-outs of his being. Nothing about him is hidden from God.

Again, let us look at the world of fallen spirits, at Satan and his hosts. Surely here, if anywhere, are purposes veiled from the eye of God. Here are plans wrapped in thick folds of darkness, away from the sight of the Almighty. But no! God sees it all. The blackest counsels of hell shine as noonday before the understanding of God. He knows it all. 'The eyes of the Lord are in every place, beholding the evil and the good' (Proverbs 15:3).

And so I might multiply examples, although there is no need to do so. But I must add this, that God knows His people. God knows everything about us, in finest detail. The hairs on our heads are numbered. Think of it! – and add to that the heads themselves, with all their longings and hopes and fears and anxieties. All is open to the sight of God. In fact, as Scripture itself tells us, His understanding is infinite (Psalm 147:5). *He* is God, and nothing escapes Him. When we have said, 'God knows everything,' we have said it all.

I find this thought overwhelming. Perhaps that shows merely that I am growing older. Youth is the time when all seems to be within the grasp of the careful student. I have left that time behind. 'I don't know' is on my lips more often now. But so also is 'God knows!' – not as a thoughtless expression in conversation, but as the conviction of my heart.

Let us make a home, then, for this thought: God knows everything. And when we have taken that fact in and given it a place at our fireside and at our table, and when we have begun to feel comfortable with it, and when we have added it to all else that we have learned about God, we may be sure it will have its effect. I think I know what that effect will be. We shall find ourselves talking to ourselves, and saying, 'Here is a God worthy to be known and proclaimed for who He is!' And we shall be right.

**B**

We may think of God's wisdom as a department of His knowledge. God's wisdom is something God knows. God, in His wisdom, knows how to choose His goals. And along with that, God knows how to attain His goals. Choosing what He wants to do, and knowing how to do it, are what we call 'the wisdom of God'. And God is full of wisdom. He has many purposes, many goals, and He knows perfectly how He will bring them about.

A Christian ought to take a special interest in the wisdom of God, for the Christian is the beneficiary of God's wisdom, not now and then, but constantly. However, I have something else in view just now. It is the way the world takes a special interest in His wisdom. God's wisdom is the one thing about God that, it seems to me, the world *openly* attacks. Men often attack God, but almost as often they try to hide their attack, even from themselves. Every sin, of course, is an assault on God. But men hide their sin from themselves. They rationalize, they find excuse; they cover over. 'Far be it from us,' they say, 'to strike a blow against God!'

*Except in the matter of wisdom.*

Listen to them:

'I don't know why God allows these wars to go on.'
'I don't know why God doesn't send rain.'
'I don't know why God didn't let us have a daughter.'
'I don't know why . . . I just don't know why!'

Now do not misunderstand me. It is a good thing to confess our ignorance. I would not want to quarrel with that. But you know as well as I do that men use these phrases, not to show how much they do not know, but to complain against God. 'Why?' is a good word, a proper word, when it asks for information. But men have found another use for it. They have learned to use it to mutter against the wisdom of God. It is as though they said, 'God would not do things this way, if He knew how badly they would work out.' They freely attack the wisdom of God.

Over against this, the Christian rejoices in the wisdom of God. Heartache comes to him as it does to all men. Puzzles about the world situation perplex him too. He has no inside information on the day-to-day acts of God. But the Christian has something better: he has faith in the wisdom of God. The Christian knows that God knows what He is doing.

It would be wrong, of course, to say that the Christian is utterly in the dark about God's purposes.

That is not true. Through the Scripture he is given knowledge that the world does not possess. Yet at best, we know but little.

Ten thousand things will happen today. I will not have time to think about even 1 per cent of these things in any detail. And those that I am able to ponder will often *seem* to go directly against the goals of God. They will not, of course, but they will seem so to me. My understanding will fail me. Nevertheless I will rest, or at least I will have every reason to rest, in the wisdom of God. I will learn to say with William Carey, 'God has His reasons.'

Now if we are not wholly in the dark, what can we say that God is doing? The Bible makes two things plain:

1) God is at work in His world, seeking His own glory.

2) God is at work in His world, seeking the good of His people. And I must add this: what God seeks to do He accomplishes. We try . . . and fail. God succeeds, not now and then, but always.

First, then, God seeks His own glory. We have been told to begin our prayers with this request, 'Hallowed be thy name' (Matthew 6:9). That gets to the heart of the matter. Right at the head of our prayer God tells us to enter into His own goal. To hallow His name is to magnify him, to show Him glorious. That is first. And He has taught us to make that our first request because it is His own first aim.

Just here is a good test of our Christianity. Do we seek His glory foremost? That is the thing the worldling cannot bring himself to do. He can sing hymns. He can give money. He can, in a rare instance, give his body to be burned. But he can do none of these things, nor anything else, for the sheer pleasure of bringing praise and glory to God.

And then there is this other thing. In all that God does, He does good to His people. Paul tells us about it:

> And we know that all things work together for good to them that love God, to them who are the called according to his purpose (Romans 8:28).

The thought is almost too great to take in: *all things* work for the good of God's people. Why? Because God makes them do so. He has power to achieve his purpose. But more than raw power is in view here. I cannot do two things at once; I lack more than power, I lack wisdom. Yet God does literally billions of things at once. If, right now, He is doing just one thing with each living person, God is doing over four billion things. Only an all-wise God could plan such a feat, let alone manage it. Here indeed is a God worthy to be known and proclaimed for who He is!

C

It is exhilarating to apply all this to missions! Why is mission work meaningful? Here is the reason: it is work that arises from the wisdom of God. The God who knows all sends us to it. God has chosen this way to bring the knowledge of Himself to the world. His choice was wise. We know that, not because we are keenly intellectual, but because He is 'the only wise God', to whom 'be honour and glory for ever and ever' (1 Timothy 1:17). That alone settles the question.

In the minds of some, however, the assurance that God is wise may be but half-formed. An imaginative story – one that perhaps you have heard before – will show you what I mean.

The scene is heaven. The Lord, we are told, has called His elect angels to hear the great thing He is about to do.

'I am sending My Son, My beloved Son, to earth.'

The angels are silent.

'There,' God goes on, 'He shall die!'

Nothing like this has been heard in heaven before.

'Why?' ventures one of the awe-struck seraphim.

'He shall die in the place of sinners, so that all who hear this good news and trust in Him shall have their sins forgiven.'

'But how shall they hear?' asks another timid voice.

'My people will go into all the world and tell them.'

Becoming bolder, an archangel spells out the question on every mind: 'What if they fail?'

For a moment there is thoughtful silence. Then God speaks 'I have no other plan.'

I do not know who made up this story. It is not hard to guess his motive. He wanted to promote missions, and he wanted to show how much hangs on our carrying out the Great Commission. He aimed to say, 'Let us get at it. Let us obey our Lord's command!' I feel sure that he did not mean to cast a shadow over the wisdom of God.

But that is what he did. For as surely as that story is told, the impression is created in the minds of some, 'God is stuck with a plan, a plan of His own choosing,

59

that will not work!' Or, at least, it has not worked. The evidence is all about us that His plan has failed. Two thousand years have gone by and the world is still not evangelized. Nor will it do to say that *men* have failed. God knew they would fail, and yet he adopted His plan. A man who carried on his business that way – ignoring foreseen difficulty – would soon be bankrupt. God is stuck with an unworkable scheme. Pity the God who says, 'I have no other plan!'

But God does not need our pity. Rather, we need His. For God to say, 'I have no other plan,' is for God to say, 'I need no other plan.' The two things are one, with God. We work on the trial-and-error method. God does not.

Why should God have some other plan? Is not this the plan that stops the mouths of angels, not only in the fantastic story above, but in Scripture? Let me show you what I mean. When Paul writes the Ephesian letter he makes this point. God, he says, has made the church,

> to the intent that now unto the principalities and powers in heavenly places might be known by the church the manifold wisdom of God (Ephesians 3:10).

That is, the angels (called here 'principalities and powers') have a lesson to learn. That lesson is God's wisdom. How are they to learn it? By looking at the church. By examining the body formed by the spread of the gospel! Here they will find the many-sided wisdom of God – here, as nowhere else. Will they see it? Do you tremble for the ark of God? Fret not: God has a plan. He does not throw up towers and rush out to meet armies without counting the cost. That kind of folly is left to men. God's plan is adequate to His task. Fear not – in His wisdom God has a plan!

That leads me to two final things. The first is this: God knows what He is doing *with you*. The Christian, the missionary, is not lost in the jungle of some vast impersonal programme, forgotten by the One who sent him. To be sure, God's programme *is* vast. It spans not only continents but eras. But it is minute as well. It extends to the trifling detail. And, most of all, it extends to you.

Here is the comfort of the missionary: he is not alone. Divine sovereignty speaks in much of the Great Commission. In it the Lord Jesus claims authority over the universe. And He lays out His orders as a King above kings. But sovereignty and wisdom speak the final word together. 'Lo, I am with you alway, even unto the end of the world' (Matthew 28:20). The missionary finds his comfort where he finds his hope of success, in the presence of his Lord.

Let me make one last point. No work on earth requires more wisdom than the work of the spread of the gospel. But if God is infinitely wise – and He is – the worker has a place to which to turn:

> If any of you lack wisdom, let him ask of God, that giveth to all men liberally, and upbraideth not; and it shall be given him (James 1:5).

James wrote these words to men whose faith was being tried. He does not specify a single trial. Rather, he speaks of diverse temptations. And what he writes is relevant to the missionary, for trials are the missionary's lot. The missionary has the tests of a common man, and he suffers the trials of a Christian. But beyond that he knows the difficulties of the greatest work on earth.

Nevertheless, let him take heart. Let him pray with Solomon, 'Give therefore thy servant an understanding heart' (1 Kings 3:9). And then let him have faith, not in the prayer, but in the God to whom it is made. For that God is the God who, from generation to generation, has stood by His people. He is the God whose knowledge and wisdom we are called to praise and proclaim.

# 6: *The Righteousness of God*

I want to come now to the righteousness or justice of God. All along in this book we have been looking at what God is like. This chapter will continue that theme, but with one difference. Here, for the first time, I want to talk about that part of God's character that may be called 'moral'. What is God like when he deals with the issues of right and wrong? How does God stand with regard to the things we term 'good' or 'evil'? What is there about God that makes these categories meaningful?

## A

It is easy enough for me to look at some man and say that he is a righteous man, or to look at some act and say that it is an unjust act. In doing that, of course, I may be simply stating my own tastes. Or, more bluntly, I may be airing my own prejudices. But we will agree, I think, that I could be saying something meaningful. Now if you hear me say such things, how can you know if I am right?

You will need to do two things. First, you will have to put aside your own prejudices as far as possible. Second, you will need some standard by which to measure. It is of no use to say, 'This man is good,' or

'That man is bad,' unless you and I have some standard against which to measure goodness and badness. Of what use is it to call a wall 'level' or 'plumb' unless we know what 'level' and 'plumb' signify?

Once when our daughter, Chris, was young she burst into a room where I sat visiting with my friend, Art. She had just finished getting dressed up.

'Mr A.,' she breathed, 'aren't I gorgeous?'

I am pretty sure she was not prepared for Art's reply. He eyed her up and down for a moment and said, 'Compared to what?'

But that is just the point, is it not? 'Compared to what?' is always the question when we speak of values. Is something or someone good, bad, level, plumb, or gorgeous? The answer must come back: compared to what?

Yet that question will not suffice when we come to God. For, you see, God *is* the standard. There is nothing beyond Him with which to compare Him. There is no measure that stands over God to which He must conform. What we know of God's character is the only rule we have for knowing what is good or bad, right or wrong. Herein lies part of the greatness of God. Moses sang,

> Ascribe ye greatness unto our God. He is the Rock, his work is perfect: for all his ways are judgment: a God of truth and without iniquity, just and right is he (Deuteronomy 32:3, 4).

What is justice? What is righteousness? They are found to perfection in God. He *is* perfect righteousness and perfect justice. Fairness and equity take their meaning from Him. If we find this troublesome it is because our thoughts of God are altogether unworthy of Him. We would like to think of God as in our own image. If we stand under a law ourselves, then, we think, so must God!

But here is the glory of God. He needs neither counsellor nor counsel. In righteousness, as in all else, He is self-sufficient. No one serves God in an advisory capacity. No law directs Him except the law of His own being. He finds all He needs within Himself. Here is the God who excites wonder and admiration and worship and praise. This is the God of whom Paul could say to his intense joy, 'whose I am and whom I serve'. (Acts 27:23). Surely He is worthy to be known!

## B

When God looks within Himself He sees righteousness. But that is no help at all to me. I cannot look directly into the being of God. For this reason He has given us His Word. If we want to know what righteousness is, we must turn to the Scriptures. We have already done so in describing what God is like. But the Bible has at least three other ways of revealing to us the righteousness of God.

The first is to show us Jesus Christ. Look at the Lord Jesus 'who knew no sin' and 'who did no sin', for, as the writer to the Hebrews tells us, Jesus Christ

'was in all points tempted like as we are, *yet without sin*' (Hebrews 4:15).

Behold the man! Read through the Gospels and you may feel the stark unlikeness between Jesus and the men around Him. You need not even compare Him with His enemies, His own disciples will illustrate the difference. Why this contrast? Because in Christ men are faced with the purity, the righteousness, of God.

Again, God gives us his commands to teach us what His righteousness is. His 'thou shalt' and his 'thou shalt not' show us what He is like, and how unlike Him we are.

Finally, God describes His acts of judgment to us. When God speaks in wrath we learn of His righteousness and justice. God is glorious in judgment!

Let us look more closely at the glory of God in judgment. The Bible develops this theme in at least three ways. First, it shows us that God judges men in the course of history. No matter how much they exalt themselves against Him, He reserves His right to bring them low. It is true that God does not always bring men to judgment in this world. Many a wicked man has lived on in the midst of luxury and ease. Yet the Bible sets before us cases where the wicked were overthrown by the hand of God. 'God is angry with the wicked every day' (Psalm 7:11), and often 'He casteth the wicked down to the ground' (Psalm 147:6).

> I will sing unto the Lord [said Moses at the Exodus], for he hath triumphed gloriously: the horse and his rider hath he thrown into the sea . . . Thy right hand, O Lord, is become glorious in power: thy right hand, O Lord, hath dashed in pieces the enemy. And in the greatness of thine excellency thou hast overthrown them that rose up against thee: thou sentest forth thy wrath, which consumed them as stubble (Exodus 15:1, 6, 7).

God's judgment in history moves Moses to song.

Second, the Bible describes a dreadful judgment in

the last hour of history. We are warned of the Day of
the Lord when all will be made right and any post-
ponement of judgment will be no more.

> Marvel not at this [said Jesus]: for the hour is coming, in
> the which all that are in the graves shall hear his voice,
> and shall come forth; they that have done good, unto the
> resurrection of life; and they that have done evil, unto the
> resurrection of damnation (John 5:28, 29).

Will God appear glorious in that day? Yes, He will.
Sit down with the Book of Revelation. Read it with
faith and prayer. Forget about identifying the two
witnesses and the seven mountains and the ten horns.
These details are not unimportant. But they are
secondary to what we are now considering.

The Book of Revelation is one of those books in the
Bible – I think also of Job and Ecclesiastes – where the
total book has a message of its own. It should be
difficult for a Christian to read Revelation without
feeling the majesty of God. Yet the effect is produced,
in the main, by watching Him at the work of judgment.

There is one last way that God shows us His glory in
judgment. It is not last in order of time. It has already
happened. But without doubt it is His highest and
brightest act of judgment. I am speaking of the
judgment against sin that God inflicted on Jesus Christ
His Son. That too was an act of glory. It was glorious
in its effects. Satan was unseated by it. The Lord Jesus
put it this way: 'The prince of this world is judged'
(John 16:11. Cf. 12:31). Notice that it is '*this*' world'
over which Satan is prince. Through Christ's death
God is forming a new world, a new creation. And He

is doing it by stripping Satan of his subjects. That is a glorious work.

But I am thinking of what the death of Christ was in itself, apart from its impact on man and Satan. It was an act of judgment. It was a display of God's righteousness. It showed just how far God would go to demonstrate His righteousness. He 'spared not his own Son' (Romans 8:32).

As soon as Jesus Christ was made 'sin for us' the wrath of God fell on Him in all its fury. We do not wonder at Christ's prayer for deliverance as He looks forward to the cross. 'If it be possible, let this cup pass from me' (Luke 22:42) seems the most natural request in the world. The wonder is in that later word, 'Nevertheless'.

> Nevertheless [Jesus prays], not as I will but as thou wilt (Matthew 26:39).

In speaking such words, Jesus consigns Himself to the unsparing justice of God. Would you know God's righteousness? See it at the cross. Hear it in the words: 'My God, my God, why hast thou forsaken me?' No answer is recorded! But the Bible does not leave us to guess the answer. It is clear. He is forsaken because He dies in the sinner's stead. That is the measure of God's hatred of sin.

Justice alone will not explain the cross. There is much more to be said. The cross was an act of love on God's part. It was an act of grace, of kindness toward lost sinners. The 'heart of God revealed'!

But our danger lies in another direction. It lies in sentimentalizing the cross. It lies in emphasizing God's grace in such a way as to slight His justice. And we can ill afford to take such a step. For in Christ's death we can read the claims of divine righteousness. Does justice demand death? Then I have a great debt and nothing with which to pay. That is a fact that cannot be sentimentalized.

I can, however, approach the cross another way. If God gave up His Son to death – and He did – He did not do it in vain. God had some great goal in view. It was that he might justly and righteously and equitably save sinners. This too is an act of justice on God's part. I do not say that it is justice to us who are saved. To us it is sheer mercy. But it is an act of justice toward Christ.

> Thou art my Son [said God to Christ] . . . Ask of me, and I shall give thee the heathen for thine inheritance, and the uttermost parts of the earth for thy possession (Psalm 2:7, 8).

So Christ asked, not by word only, but by laying down His life.

And the Father answers with joy. From every tribe and tongue and kindred and nation God gives His Son the men Christ purchased. It is in perfect justice that He does so. Both in judgment and in mercy God acts righteously. His righteous acts give us a glimpse of His glory. And seeing that, we say it once more: here is a God worthy to be known and proclaimed for who He is.

The Christian worker may find himself asking, 'What am I doing here?' (wherever 'here' may be). 'Why am I doing this and that?' I have tried to answer these questions by saying that 'God' is the only satisfactory answer. The first thing that strikes us is the fact that God commands missions. And that is sufficient reason for being involved.

Yet we may go further, and add to the command a fuller knowledge of the God who sends us. And that is what we ought to do. We ought to seek clearer views of the God we serve. That will make our work meaningful when success escapes us.

Think about Isaiah. God sent him on a mission of judgment, of condemnation. I doubt whether he liked his assignment. I certainly would not have liked it. Paul was glad to say of his own ministry, 'we are the savour of life,' as well as 'the savour of death'. But Isaiah could not speak in that way. He was sent to 'make the heart of this people fat, and make their ears heavy, and shut their eyes' (Isaiah 6:10).

How does a man get ready for such a ministry? God gave Isaiah a vision of Himself. Isaiah was made to see the holiness of God. He was made to know the contrast between himself and God.

And that was enough. That was his preparation, he was ready without a command, with just a hint from God. Listen to him tell it:

Also I heard the voice of the Lord, saying, Whom shall I send, and who will go for us? Then said I, Here am I; send me (Isaiah 6:8).

It was a difficult mission. But then, Isaiah had a new view of God with which to meet it.

The missionary often lives where the righteousness of God is challenged. It may be the people who deny it. It may be events that make it seem that God has forgotten to be just. The challenge may come from some totally unexpected quarter. But it will come. Let me give you an example.

I have recently seen a missionary film. In it a native woman was buried alive. The woman, dead by native standards but still breathing, was a friend of the missionary. As you may well imagine, the missionary did all she could do to stop the burial. But it made no difference. The earth received the body. The grave was closed. And the missionary was left distraught.

I do not pretend that I could have taken that sight any better than the missionary did. Nothing that I can think of could reduce the dreadfulness of that scene. And yet—. And yet I had the feeling that something was missing from the film. Not in all parts of it, but at this point. For a brief instant we were left without God. Perhaps that was the very effect intended. It may be that the film-maker wanted to help us taste the same desolate emptiness. But I do know this, that I wanted to stand up, then and there, to vindicate the ways of God. I wanted to declare the sovereignty of God so that the audience would not be left to think that what they saw was mere chance. And I wanted to expound the justice of God. I wanted to answer Abraham's question, 'Shall not the Judge of all the earth do right?' (Genesis 18:25). I wanted to say that we were not witnessing an accident. Heathenism is a judgment from Almighty God. It is more than misfortune. To be a heathen and to practise their customs is condemnation from the righteous God. The Judge of all the earth overlooks nothing. And the Judge of all the earth, everywhere and to everyone, always does right.

Does this seem like strong meat? I am sure it does. But the Christian worker must not shrink from eating it. It will do him good in two ways. First, it will set the tone for his teaching. From the first his listeners will be made to see God as He is. What greater boon could they receive? I know of none. The truth about God will not turn them away if God means to save them. The truth is His instrument.

And then there is something else. I am thinking of the effect that the truth will have on the missonary's own mind. Let him get a firm hold on the righteousness of God. Let him keep it before his mind's eye. And, most of all, let him apply it to his own life.

I think I know the result. It comes to me forcefully as I write. No man who rightfully calls himself a Christian can fail to see it. *Salvation is only and always by the grace of God.*

Was I better than the heathen who perish? I would be a fool to think so. Nor was the missionary. We were blind and deaf. We were haters of God. Most of us sinned against more light in a year than the heathen do in their lifetime. God had no reason to save us – none, that is, but His own goodness and grace.

So here is our motive for service. Is there a righteous God in heaven who will nevertheless save men like us? Who knows, then, but that He will also save our hearers? Is there a just God who will save men like we and they are? Is there a God who bases salvation on both grace and righteousness? Then here is a God who is a wonder. Here is a God whom we can adore when we cannot understand. Here is a God whom we can serve, a God who Himself tells us that He is 'a just God and a Saviour' (Isaiah 45:21).

# 7: *The Graciousness of God*

The close of the last chapter brought us to the subject of the grace of God. I want to pick up that thread once more. To the Christian there is no thought more precious than the thought of God's goodness and grace. If there is a stern side to the doctrine of God, there is a compassionate side as well. There is a tenderness in the character of God that may be threatened by an over-emphasis on His justice and power. Let us see if we can strike the right balance.

**A**

If a man has come to the place where he is seriously interested in the work of missions it must already be a fixed principle with him that God is good. Missions makes no sense on any other basis. If we knew enough, perhaps, we might prove the goodness of God from any of the events that presently startle and confuse us. But that is beyond us. We will be content with what the Scriptures reveal. May the Lord help us to be gripped by what we find!

We know God's goodness by several Bible words. The word we like best is 'love'. Others are 'mercy', 'compassion', 'kindness', and 'grace'. Each of these terms has its own flavour. But we ought not to distinguish them too closely. The context, not the word used, is usually the best clue to any shade of difference.

To speak rightly of God's love we will need a definition. In Greek and Hebrew (the two main Bible languages), as in English, there is no one meaning of 'love' that will fit each and every place where the word is used. But, generally, we may be said to love others when we desire to benefit them, when we desire to promote their interest.

In this sense God loves His creation. The Psalmist says,

> The Lord is good to all: and his tender mercies are over all his works (Psalm 145:9).

God desires to benefit His creation, and He does so. We cannot doubt His power. Here we learn also that God has the will.

What God does reveals what God is. That is the important point. God *does* good because God *is* good. His tender mercies do not hide His character. They make it manifest. That does not mean, of course, that we recognize His every act of mercy. Some mercies baffle us. That is a common experience in life. But it does mean that, as surely as we find God's act of kindness, we may be sure that there is a God of kindness behind the act. Every man may discover this facet of God's character if he will. Jesus taught us that it takes no more than sunshine and rain to show us the goodness of God if we have eyes to see it.

It is true, however, that God does not do good to all men equally. Again, the rain and the sunshine will show this truth. Some men live where the amount of

74

rain poses a health problem. Others live in drought conditions. Neither can live without sunshine and rain. But each could use more of one and less of the other.

This fact is so plain that it would require a word from God to contradict it. But the Scripture confirms it. And it does so in matters even more important than sunshine and rain. Note, for instance, how Moses explained the Exodus. And keep in mind that the Exodus meant the difference between slavery and freedom:

> The Lord did not set his love upon you, nor choose you, because ye were more in number than any people; for ye were the fewest of all people: but because the Lord loved you, and because he would keep the oath which he had sworn unto your fathers, hath the Lord brought you out with a mighty hand, and redeemed you out of the house of bondmen, from the hand of Pharaoh king of Egypt (Deuteronomy 7:7, 8).

Freedom and slavery are in the hand of the Lord. So also are rain and sunshine. And they are given to some, as an act of love on God's part, in greater measure than they are given to others.

Nowhere is this more clearly seen than in salvation. God gives His saving grace to some and not to others. Why am I a Christian when my neighbour is not? Let me see. Was it *my* wisdom or righteousness or love that moved God to save me? None of these, of course! It was something in God, not something in me. I was not wise enough or righteous enough to turn to Christ. I did not seek Him; He sought me. I did not love Him; He loved me. I was not fair with my Maker, but He was much more than fair with me. Whether salvation is seen as mercy (that is, loving help to the needy) or as grace (that is, loving aid to the undeserving), it is all of God. And God gives this love as He pleases.

'But wait,' someone says, 'doesn't this make God partial? And doesn't the Scripture teach that God is no respecter of persons? How can this be, if God loves some more than others?' These are fair questions. And the Bible answers them. The answer lies in defining 'partial'.

When are we said to be partial? Partiality starts when we find something in a person or group of persons that we especially like.

'I like economic and political power,' says one.

'I'm drawn to intelligence and wit,' says another.

'I am captivated by beauty,' says a third.

That is the beginning.

But there is another step in partiality. It comes when we show favour to certain persons based on what we like about them. Many of us are partial to members of our own schools or political parties. And our partiality to our families is a proverb. Blood, we say, is thicker than water.

Now, in this way, God is not partial toward men at all, for among fallen men God finds no goodness to admire. The thing that God would be drawn to, namely, godlikeness, does not exist, except where He creates it. He does not elect this man, and that woman, on the basis of anything He finds in them. In that sense, God is not a respecter of persons. He is not partial.

All this points up a crucial difference between God's love and ours, and we must not overlook it. Some 700 years ago Thomas Aquinas explained the difference in a way I cannot improve upon. Here are his words:

> God does not love as we love . . . Our will is not the cause of the good in what we love. We are induced to love by good which exists already . . . With God it is the reverse. When God wills some good to one whom he loves, his will is the cause of this good being in him . . .

There is nothing in us to induce God to love us, or to be partial to us. Faced with that situation, however, God has not abandoned His world. He has loved His world; He has planned much good for all His creatures. And He has chosen to be nothing less than a Father to a multitude. As Father He creates great good where He could never have found it. To His children He gives likeness to Christ, and this is His choicest gift. It reveals His love 'to the uttermost'.

### B

Do you use the word 'epiphany'? In some circles it is quite well known. In others, including my own, it is little used. 'Epiphany' is taken over almost unchanged into English from the Greek New Testament. It means 'an appearance'. Among Christians it is used to refer to the coming or appearance of Jesus Christ in this world, and is used in its verbal form in the following places:

Titus 2:11 – The grace of God that bringeth salvation *hath appeared* . . .
Titus 3:4 – The kindness and love of God our Saviour toward man *appeared* . . .

In both verses 'epiphany' is joined with words that tell of God's goodness: 'grace', 'kindness', and 'love'.

Now here is what interests me about these verses. Both are about the coming of Jesus Christ, yet neither of them mentions Him by name. Paul does not say, 'Christ appeared'. He says 'grace' or 'kindness and love appeared.' Does Paul mean to tell us that these three words are simply other names for Jesus? That is not exactly Paul's meaning.

The Christian position is this: God has always loved men, but it is Christ crucified who best expresses that love. He proves it beyond all doubt. It is not that the grace and kindness and love of God had never been seen before. Noah and others found grace in the eyes of the Lord. But a comparison is made. Compared to the life and death of Jesus Christ, all other displays of God's love – great as they have been – are as nothing. John speaks in the same way.

> The law was given by Moses, [he tells us] but grace and truth came by Jesus Christ (John 1:17).

Note that this is a historical statement, not a timeless one. It does not mean that all the grace that men have ever enjoyed came by Jesus Christ. That may be true, but it is not the truth set forth here.

John means that a new era has come, the era of grace. Grace manifested, grace shouted from the house-tops – that is what this new age is about! And it comes in the only way it could come. It comes by Christ. God determined to say 'grace' and 'kindness' and 'love' in a deeper, richer way than He had ever done before. So He said, 'Jesus!' Or, through Paul, 'Christ crucified!'

God's love is especially connected with the cross.
John tells us again,

> In this was manifested the love of God toward us,
> because that God sent his only begotten Son into the
> world, that we might live through him. Herein is love,
> not that we loved God, but that he loved us, and sent
> his Son to be the propitiation for our sins (1 John
> 4:9,10).

Here we see the love of God at its highest. God sends
His Son. And God sends His Son to be a 'propitiation'.
That is, God sends Him as an offering to turn away
God's own wrath from sinners. God's wrath falls on
Christ at the cross, so that sinners may go free. A
Welsh miner neatly summed it up by saying: 'He
swapped with me!'

This has been often misunderstood. Some have
thought, or professed to think, that Christianity speaks
of a loving Christ and a wrathful God. But if we let the
Bible take us by the hand we will not think so. God the
Father sent His Son. And in sending Him He showed
us what His own goodness and love were like. At the
cross, on the head of the Lord Jesus, wrath and love
meet. Both are God's. But the wrath falls that God
might express His love. The wrath is a means to that
end. John might have written, 'Herein is wrath . . . ,'
but he did not. John looks beyond the cross to the God
behind it. Seeing Him he says, 'Herein is *love* . . . he
*loved* us, and sent his Son . . .'

C

Now we must ask: 'In what way does God's goodness

bear on the subject of missions?'[1] To begin an answer to that question we look at John 10:17, 18. Jesus is speaking:

> 'Therefore doth my Father love me, because I lay down my life, that I might take it again'. No man taketh it from me, I lay it down of myself. I have power to lay it down, and I have power to take it again. This commandment have I received of my Father.'

Most of us would not be bold enough to try to tell in one short phrase why God the Father has loved the Lord Jesus. The task would be quite beyond us. It seems impossible. Yet that is what Jesus has done here. 'Therefore doth my Father love me,' He says, 'because I lay down my life.' The word 'therefore' brings the love and goodness and compassion of God into the closest connection with missions. Let me explain what I mean.

Why does the Father love the Lord Jesus? The answer lies in the death of Christ, but not as an end in itself. Christ's death was the means to accomplish what the Triune God had purposed, that is to say, the salvation of men given to the Son by the Father. And the obedience of the Son at tremendous cost to Himself prompts the Father's love. In other words, the Father loved the Son precisely because the Son was pursuing what we would call 'the missionary vision.' That is why Jesus laid down His life. His being a missionary required it.

It must be said, however, that Jesus was a missionary in a way in which we cannot follow Him. We have no

1. I am indebted for much of the material in the following pages to a sermon entitled 'The Sacrifice of Christ the Type and Model of Missionary Effort,' by James H. Thornwell. See his *Collected Writings*, vol. II, pp. 409ff.

spotless lives to give. We cannot bear the sins of mankind. We cannot purchase forgiveness for ourselves, much less for others. All of that is true, and we must not forget it. It is not the whole truth, however. We must say more. Behind the act of Christ lay His motives. And here we may follow Him, even to death if necessary. His motives must be ours as well.

What were Christ's motives? First, His love for the Father. Christ admires the justice of God in punishing sin. As an act of worship He allows Himself to bear that punishment. No, more! 'He allows Himself' is too passive. Christ takes the punishment for sin upon Himself. And He does so because He loves and admires the Father who punishes Him! Here is love to adore for ever!

We must follow the Lord Jesus here. Thornwell puts it this way:

> The real difficulty [of the heathen] is their reluctance to glorify His name . . . God is glorious; the Christian man knows it, and he wants all the world to know it, and his anxiety to spread the truth is in proportion to the enormity of the lie which is supplanting it . . . The spontaneous dictate of love is to maintain the rights and vindicate the worth of the object to which it is directed. (pp. 429–431).

If I do not admire the love of God in Christ I have no right to call myself a Christian. I may take the name 'Christian', but I have emptied it of a chief part of its meaning. My profession is a farce. I had better drop it, and face reality.

If I am a God-admirer, however, the indifference of the world to God's glory must wound me. It is robbery.

When the heathen bow the knee to anything less than the Lord of heaven they steal the renown that pertains to God. Can I bear to see them bestow it on their idols? Surely not! The glory of God's love, and of all else that He is, belongs to God alone!

So then, love for God's character, including His grace and goodness, must move me. If I am grieved that men suppress the knowledge of God I must respond. That much is clear, but what must I do?

Here is what I must do: I must adopt the stance of my Saviour. I must follow Him here especially. Jesus well understood the depths of man's sin in casting off God. He felt it and suffered its intensity. In part, that explains the cross. With the Psalmist Jesus could say, 'The reproaches of them that reproached thee are fallen upon me' (Psalm 16:9). And through it all He kept His zeal for God's glory. Through it all He worshipped the Father.

But how did Jesus react to His tormentors? Did He call down fire from heaven? He did not! Instead, we hear Him pray, 'Father, forgive them; for they know not what they do' (Luke 23:34).

A cynic might ask, 'Where, now, is Jesus' zeal for God? Does He not know that they hate Him because they hate His Father? Or, does He not care? If He loved His Father He would destroy these wicked men!' Many would not follow Jesus here at all. But we must follow Him. For the Lord Jesus the finest and noblest and grandest way to celebrate the love of His Father was to reduce rebels to friendship with God. And the cross was the way to do it. The same cross upon which divine wrath fell! Zeal for the glory of God *was* foremost with our Lord.

**The Graciousness of God**

Another motive in Jesus is pity and compassion for lost men. If we are to follow Him this must be our motive as well. And when we combine reverence for God with compassion toward men we will see ourselves called to whatever sacrifice is necessary, just as Jesus did. As Thornwell says again:

> It would be contrary to the whole analogy of our religion . . . to suppose that those . . . whose great business is to die, should be remitted to indolence and ease. They are called to sacrifice. Hence, it does not stagger my faith to be told of the magnitude of the enterprise and the comparative inefficiency of the means . . . of the obstinate and bitter prejudices which must be subdued . . . the cruel persecutions which must be endured . . . All these and a thousand more such obstructions are only proofs that the Church must tread in the footsteps of her Master, and bless the nations by the sacrifice of her own ease and life. (pp. 437, 8).

The goodness of God has sent the Lord Jesus with a vision for missions. In pursuit of that mission Jesus has died. Again, the grace of God now sends us with that same vision. Perhaps we too shall die in following it. But whether we die or live is not important; in one sense of the word we are dead already (Colossians 3:3). What is important is to know that, whether by life or by death, we must respond to God's goodness and mercy in the way the Lord Jesus has set before us. Let us worship God for all that He is. Let us extol His grace and kindness toward sinners. Let us be jealous for His glory.

And, finally, let us be convinced, as Jesus was, that the best and brightest way to celebrate God's grace is so to act that His enemies are led to become His

83

friends. Here is an aim worthy of any sacrifice. It will mean the eternal happiness of men and women. A man might well die with that object in view!

But it will mean much more. To see the world's rebels turned into friends of God is, after all, a God-centred goal. It looks beyond benefit to men. For in coming to Christ their hearts will be changed. They will be made new men throughout. As friends they will do what they would not do as foes. They will lay down their arms and raise their songs of praise: they will *worship* their Creator. They will adore Him whom they once despised. They will praise the Lord!

Nor is that all. They will not do these things without us. On the contrary, for ever we shall have the pleasure of hearing them join us in our worship. For ever we will say together what I have tried to say all through this book: our God is worthy to be known and proclaimed for who He is!

# 8: *God in His Faithfulness*

In the first section of this book I have tried to emphasize some of the attributes of God. This chapter will close this section. But there is one thing more about God that I want us to look at, namely, God's faithfulness. If I am to get the good of the gospel and share it with others, there is one thing more I must depend on. I must lean on the faithfulness of God.

**A**

When I was a Boy Scout we sometimes had to tell what a Scout was like. And we had a set form of words for doing it. We would say, 'A Scout is trustworthy, loyal, helpful . . .', and so on, through a long list of endowments which no one was to doubt that we possessed! We ended up with 'brave, clean, and reverent'.

I wonder now if the order of those words was significant. Probably not, for most of them. Yet I think it likely that 'reverent' came last to leave us with the reminder that we belonged to God.

Right now, however, I want us to look at that first word. Why does 'trustworthy' head the list? It could be mere chance. Probably the author wanted to start well, to provide a leading indicator of what a young man should be. If that was the case, he made a fine choice. To say that a boy or girl or man or woman is 'trustworthy' is, to my mind, high praise indeed. When we say that, we mean that he keeps his word. You can count on what he says.

Now that is the first thing we mean when we talk of the faithfulness of God. We mean: you can trust God to keep His word. You can count on what He says. If you can find even one thing that God has committed Himself to, you can be sure that it will be done. God is trustworthy. God is faithful. My confidence has no power of its own. My trust rests on His trustworthiness. My faith is pillowed on the faithfulness of God.

Someone has sung, 'Every promise in the Book is mine.' But that is not so, and for this we should be thankful. Some of those promises are promises of judgment. A threat, we know, is a promise of sorts, but it is one from which every hearer desires to steer clear.

But we might rightly sing, 'Every promise in the Book is true.' Or, to be more exact, 'Every promise made by God in the Book is true.' Satan promised Eve, 'Ye shall not surely die, but be as gods,' if she ate the fruit. That promise, though 'in the Book', is a lie. But God's words, rightly understood, never fail. They do not; and they can not. God is pledged to fulfil them.

The Lord Jesus said, 'Man shall not live by bread alone, but by every word that proceedeth out of the mouth of God' (Matthew 4:4). In saying that, He was saying nothing new, for it is a timeless truth. Just as we depend on bread to maintain our bodies, so also we must rely on Scripture to support our spirits. The spirit needs truth to live, as the body needs food. But where shall we find truth? Who speaks faithful words? God does – in His Book! God is ever faithful to His Word.

**B**

Then, again, God is faithful to His people. That is the second thing that God's faithfulness means. These two truths – God's faithfulness to His Word and to His people – are closely related. But there is a personal touch in the one that is not so obvious in the other. A threat of judgment, for example, is personal enough, but you could hardly call it a 'touch'. It is more like a blow in the face. When we speak of God's faithfulness to His people we introduce a note of tenderness, a note that may be missing elsewhere.

Here is a tale that will show what I am getting at. It dramatizes God's faithfulness to His people. I want to tell it my own way, but it is based on another man's story. The author, however, is unknown.

A Christian dreamed that he was walking along a beach with the Lord. The beach, he soon realized, represented the course of his life. Scanning the sands behind him he relived scene after scene of his earlier years. It was the sight of the footprints that awakened his memories. As far back as he could see there were two sets of footprints, his own and those of his Lord.

And yet, that was not quite true. Here and there he saw but one set of footprints in the sand. He saw, too, that the single trail of footsteps went through some of the saddest, most difficult moments of his life.

Turning to the Lord, he raised a question. 'Lord,' he said, 'did I fail to understand You? I thought You

87

had promised never to forsake me, not even for a moment. But look and see the places where there is only one set of footprints. Why did You leave me when I needed You most?'

There was stillness for some minutes. It had taken the man a good deal of courage to ask his question, and before he was done he had dropped his eyes to the ground. At first he dared not look up. Then, in the quietness, he regained his nerve. Finally he stole a glance at the Lord. He was unprepared for what he saw.

The Lord was smiling.

'My child,' the Lord said gently, 'I love you and I would not leave you. But you are right. There are places with but one set of footprints. And those were your hardest times. That is why *your* footprints are not there. You see, it was then that I carried you.'

That tale is not from the Bible, but no matter, it teaches us Bible truth. Has the Lord said, 'I will never leave thee, nor forsake thee' (Hebrews 13:5)? Then He will not. The lesson of the story is that often God is most really present with His people when they least feel His presence. Would not Jacob's son, Joseph, say the same? Would not Job? And will not you and I, when we look back from glory? Yes, we will say, 'Jesus led me all the way.' We do not always feel it now, but we shall know it then. We shall know it because God is faithful.

We put this in another way when we say that God does not get weary. He does not nod off while at His job. If that seems like a bold figure you may blame the Psalmist. After looking about him for help, he says,

'My help cometh from the Lord, which made heaven and earth. He will not suffer thy foot to be moved: he that keepeth thee will not slumber. Behold, he that keepeth Israel shall neither slumber nor sleep' (Psalm 121:2-4).

God follows His own counsel: 'Be not weary in well doing!' Night and day, summer and winter, God's faithfulness is toward His people.

## C

Finally, God is faithful to His own first goal. Throughout the universe and throughout history, God seeks His own glory. He will not be sidetracked; God will glorify Himself. You may count on it. This too is the faithfulness of God.

God had regard to His own glory when He formed the worlds. That is why 'the heavens declare the glory of God.' They were made to do so. It is a passion with God's creation to praise Him. The stones are prepared to cry out at a moment's notice. Thunder announces His majesty.

> Give unto the Lord the glory due unto his name . . .
> The voice of the Lord is upon the waters: the God of glory
> thundereth . . . (Psalm 29:2, 3).

Angels and men must see the glory of the Creator in the fury of the storm. Nature reveals God to those with eyes to see Him.

Again, God had His own glory in mind when He fashioned man. That is the first thing to get clear. Do not think that a man, any man, is an end in himself. Not at all! He exists for the glory of God. We see that in the opening chapter of Scripture. Man is made in

89

the image of God. Wherever man goes he will display the nature of God in miniature. And he will carry out God's design. He may stand and swear that there is no God, but never mind. His 'chief end is to glorify God' – and he will do so.

Of course, to glorify God and to aim at His glory are no longer the same thing. The fall is the dividing line. Before man sinned, he aimed at God's glory. Now he does not. Yet, as we have seen, the fall does not cause God's purpose to fail. God has many unwilling servants. They are not only unprofitable, but wicked. They are His servants, nevertheless.

There is one thing more that God has made for his glory, namely, the new creation. When men are born again they are remade. 'We are [God's] workmanship,' said Paul, 'created in Christ . . .' (Ephesians 2:10). Believers are 'a kind of firstfruits', a down payment on the future world where all things will again seek to honour God. Are you a Christian? God has made you anew that you

> should shew forth the praises of him who hath called you out of darkness into his marvellous light (1 Peter 2:9).

And He has given you a heart to do it. A Christian has a 'heart of flesh,' that is to say, a responsive heart, a heart set on glorifying God. .

The old creation and the new are both made for God, and both advance God's glory. They do it, however, in diverse ways, and in ways past finding out, in this life at least. We must adore where we cannot understand. Understanding is good; we do not despise it. But adoration is better; let us not neglect it. Paul has said of God that 'of him, and through him, and to him, are all things: to whom be glory for ever. Amen.' (Romans 11:36).

1) 'Of him . . . are all things.' God is the source of all that exists.

2) 'Through him . . . are all things.' God is the sustainer of all things.

3) 'To him . . . are all things.' All things exist for God's purposes and glory.

When we can receive those three truths we are on our way to the knowledge of God. But there is one thing better. We take a giant step forward, when we can add with Paul: 'To whom be glory for ever. Amen!'

## D

It seems odd to ask the question, 'How does the faithfulness of God bear on world missions?' The answer would have to be, 'In more ways than we can possibly imagine.' Perhaps someone, somewhere, might suggest a way of thinking of God that does not impinge on missions. I do not know what it could be. God's faithfulness touches everything. We cannot think 'missions' apart from the conviction that God is faithful, that God can be absolutely trusted.

Is God faithful to His word? We know that He is faithful, and we know that this is the basis of missions. In fact, it is the missionary vision of God that gave us the Scriptures. If it had pleased God, the fall of man might have brought an end to man's story. Man was ripe for destruction. Had God destroyed the race, no Scripture would ever have been written.

But God had a vision, a vision for missions. It focused on the sending of His Son. So, just at the outset of fallen man's history, God spoke to Eve of better things to come. Her descendants would do agelong battle with Satan's kin. Yet the outcome could not be in doubt. A 'seed' would come, Jesus Christ, who would land the killing blow on the old serpent himself. And it is our joy to look back at that promise and to know that God was faithful to that word. We were not there through the dark ages of pre-Christian history. We were not there to know of His promise nor to respond in faith. We might have signally failed to trust if we had been there. But God was faithful. God was as good as His word.

Long years passed and in God's good time, He sent His promised Son. 'Ye shall be witnesses unto me,' Jesus promised his first followers. And they were. 'Lo, I am with you alway,' He said to them. And He is. We find the evidence in such statements as these:

> And the Lord added to the church daily such as should be saved (Acts 2:47).
> Many of them which heard the word believed; and the number of the men was about five thousand (Acts 4:4).
> And believers were the more added to the Lord, multitudes both of men and women (Acts 5:14).

Open success does not always follow the preaching of the gospel. It would be a mistake to think so – and very discouraging as well. But when men do become worshippers of God and believers in Jesus Christ, there we have tangible evidence that Christ is as good as His word.

And, of course, God *remains* faithful to His people. That, too, is a basis of missions. Do we want success? God promises it to all His people. Not the success of

92

our service; in service we may be 'the savour of life unto life' or 'the savour of death unto death.' God will give or withhold the increase as it pleases Him. Yet, in another sense, we shall certainly succeed.

God is more interested in our sanctification than He is in our service. Let us get that clear. It explains much else, including many of our apparent failures. No God-sent missionary who believes in Jesus Christ *is allowed* to call himself a failure!

This does not mean that a missionary is a special breed of Christian. To change from his native land and culture to another does not place a halo on the head of the Christian worker. No one knows that better than the missionary himself. If others make that mistake, he is not likely to do so.

What I mean is this. In speaking of success and failure we are right at the heart of what being a Christian is about. God is determined to *save* His people in the fullest sense of that term. Salvation means a great deal more than to keep a sinner out of hell! The New Testament shows that it means most of all to remake a man or a woman to be like the Lord Jesus. And God intends to do just that. In Paul's words, we are predestined 'to be conformed to the image of his Son' (Romans 8:29).

'But,' someone asks, 'you don't mean to say that a Christian is automatically successful, do you? Sanctification is not automatic, is it?' No, of course it is not. It is not *automatic*, but—.

Let me ask a question. What sort of picture comes to your mind when you hear the word 'automatic'? I cannot answer for you, but to me 'automatic' calls up the world of machinery and gadgetry. Automatic

93

pencils come to mind, automatic doors, and, on a larger scale, automatic machine tools, gears that mesh with other gears – that kind of thing! Cold, hard, *impersonal*! That is it, isn't it? Certain, but impersonal – that is what 'automatic' suggests to me.

When we speak of sanctification we are speaking of another world, the world of personal relationships. Here we leave doors and tools and gears behind. Here we have certainties, but they are of a different kind.

'I am sure my wife will not betray me,' says a man. Why is he sure? Does he have her locked away? Does he have her on a leash? Or has he done some third or fourth absurd mechanical thing to her? To ask these questions is to answer them. They are ridiculous. The man is certain, but it is not 'automatic'. The certainty is moral, not mechanical.

So it is also with the Christian. God has given the believer a bent to please Him. And the Christian does so. He does not obey perfectly, but he characteristically seeks to please God. That is what a Christian is like. That is what a missionary is like, as well. It is often 'two steps forward and one step back.' But that is progress, it is not defeat. And, it is God's gift. It is the faithfulness of God. That is why the God-sent missionary is forbidden to say, 'I am a failure.' Instead, with all his faults, he is the continuing workmanship of God.

And that brings me to my last point. God's highest goal is to seek His own glory. God is faithful to that goal, and He will surely attain it. He will not be sidetracked. The work of missions, the work of salvation is based on this goal. Here are God's words through Isaiah.

> Look unto me, and be ye saved, all the ends of the
> earth: for I am God, and there is none else. I have sworn
> by myself, the word is gone out of my mouth in right-
> eousness, and shall not return, that unto me every knee
> shall bow . . . (Isaiah 45:22, 23).

Note the connection: 'be ye saved' and 'every knee
shall bow'. Yes, others shall also bow, others who are
not saved. And that too will bring God glory. It will
glorify His justice.

But here is the point. God has gone into the world
to get glory to Himself. He has set His heart on doing
it by saving a multitude of men and boys, women and
girls, from one end of the globe to the other. It has not
pleased Him to do all the work alone. Instead, God has
formed a team of men and women to serve Him. The
missionary is part of that team. He may seem to be
nothing more than that. But he is nothing less.

That team spans the ages and the continents. At any
given moment we can say little about its success. Here
a team-mate is injured and carried from the field.
There the opposition is pushing them backward, not
forward. That is the way it is – *at any given moment*.

But there is a broader view. It is this: God's team is
the winning team. Never mind the setbacks. They will
come. But as surely as God is God, His team is the
winning team. in the most discouraging place on earth,
and at the most disheartening hour, the cause is never
in doubt. Of what other cause can this be said? None
on this earth; not one! The missionary is engaged in
this world's only sure pursuit. Let him take heart. His
resolve can never be in vain. He serves the royal
Master, the victorious Prince.

Wherever the God-sent missionary is, whatever he

95

is doing, however low he appears in his own sight and in the eye of the world – all of that counts for nothing against him. His life does not take its meaning from such things. His significance lies elsewhere. It lies in the fact that he is a servant of God, the God who is faithful to His word, to His people, and to His own glory. That God is the One worthy to be known and served and loved and followed and proclaimed for ever. Not for his rewards – God Himself is the reward. He is worthy to be known and proclaimed for who He is. His faithfulness proves it.

# 9: 'Glory . . . in the Face of Jesus Christ'

This chapter is transitional. It links together the two themes that I promised to deal with before the book reaches its close. Let me remind you what they are. In the preface I said I would aim to show you that:

1) *God is worthy to be known and proclaimed for who He is, and that fact is an important part of the missionary motive and message.*

2) *Those who know the most about God are the most responsible and best equipped to tell of Him.*

So far I have dealt with the first aim. I have striven to speak of God as the Scripture reveals Him. I have sought to show how God's character bears on missions. I have tried to point out that the knowledge of God is, in fact, the Christian's greatest reward. Here is motive and message enough for any man.

It has not been at all difficult to illustrate these truths from the Bible. These things, of course, are a large part of what the Bible is about. Scripture is the book of God in more than one sense. It is God's book because God is its author. But it is also His book because it reveals who He is. In the Bible God has given us Himself!

In this chapter I want to make a point that comes out of my illustrations. Up to now I have taken my illustrations from both God and Christ in order to give a full-orbed view of what God is like. But I have frequently concentrated on God the Father. For example, I had the Father in view in speaking of God's sovereignty. To show God's sovereignty from the life of Christ would not be impossible. But it would make us focus on what was exceptional in the life of Jesus. He came as a servant. He served both His Father and the men around Him. Sovereignty was not inconsistent with the Lord Jesus' servitude, but His submission was much more obvious.

So also with self-sufficiency. As God, the Lord Jesus was self-sufficient. But surely He laid aside the glory of that attribute when He came to earth. Instead He became our example. We did not need an example of self-sufficiency. We needed something else. It is from Jesus that we learn dependence on God the Father and on the Holy Spirit. It seemed best, then, to find the illustrations of God's self-sufficiency elsewhere. That is what I have done. But in doing so I have laid us open to a danger. That is what I must now discuss.

## A

The danger is that we may forget that the man who knows God best is the man who best knows Jesus Christ. It is good and right that we study what God is like. That study takes us throughout the Scriptures. And we must search them from beginning to end. But we must do more. We must fully expect to find the high point of God's revelation in His Son. We must keep our eye fixed on Jesus Christ.

In the following chapters I will be speaking, as I have intimated, to 'those who know the most about

God'. But we must be clear as to their identity. We must also strive to be among them. To do that we must remain clear of the temptation I am about to describe.

Imagine yourself looking around the evangelical world. In some ways the sight is not encouraging. One reason is that our knowledge of God seems in short supply. The books Christians read indicate as much. Prophecy is a major interest just now. So is the subject of human relations. We have lots of 'how-to' books. And 'pop biography' is strong. But who has read *The Sovereignty of God* by Arthur Pink, or *The Knowledge of the Holy* by A. W. Tozer? Comparatively few!

Yet perhaps we have read them, or books like them. Shall we then look down our noses at our fellow Christians? Shall we count ourselves among those 'who know the most about God'? 'No!' we say. 'Of course not!' We are indignant at the very thought!

But we must delve more deeply into the matter.

In the questions I have just asked there are two things to which we might react. The first is the blunt language I have used. The second is the content. But these two things are quite different. We have learned to respond negatively to the words 'look down our noses at'. We have been taught that one must never 'look down his nose at' anybody. And we have been told that, if we count ourselves as members of some élite group (such as 'those who know the most about God'), it is best to let others sing our praises. Modesty compels it. Either of these lessons makes it almost certain that we will give a vehement 'No!' to my questions.

But we may say 'no' as indignantly as possible and

99

still fail to come to terms with the content of what I have asked.

How could we make such a mistake? Very simply! All we need to do is to fail to grasp one truth. That truth is this: the glory of God is best seen in the person and work of Jesus Christ. It is true that the evangelical world no longer majors on the doctrine of God. And it is true that we all are losers thereby. But for some of us the temptation lies in another direction. It lies in learning the great truths concerning God as He is revealed apart from Jesus Christ and forgetting that the Lord Jesus is the key to the knowledge of God. If we do that, we are not 'those who know the most about God', but those who know the least.

Jesus said, 'Ye shall be witnesses *unto me*' (Acts 1:8). He did not mean that exclusively, as though we are to neglect all else in God's Word. Of course not! We must mine the whole Scripture, even in evangelism. There are no truths that we must hold back when we seek to bring men to Christ. They must hear both what pleases them and what does not please them. But we must have a focal point for ourselves and for our message. That point is Jesus Christ. It is not simply God's character. It is the character of God as He is revealed in our Saviour. It is *God in Christ*. Any other focus disqualifies us.

### B

Let me see if I can apply this.

First, we must learn to think of the Old Testament as a forward-looking book. I believe that two things often get in our way when we try to do this. First, the sheer bulk of the Old Testament may defeat us. Since the fulfilment of the hope is more glorious than the promise, we might have expected the fulfilment to be told in many more words. But that is not what we find.

The other thing is this. The forward look in the Old Testament is often in the background. It is more implicit than explicit. It flavours the text when the text itself seems to be ignoring the distant future. This, of course, is not always the case. God tells us plainly enough about the future when He chooses to do so. But that is the exception, not the rule.

Often this has come home to me when reading Luke 24:27. There Luke says,

> And beginning at Moses and all the prophets, [Jesus] expounded to them in all the scriptures the things concerning himself.

In reading the words I have said to myself, 'I wish I could have been there. I wonder what the Lord said.' And in earlier years I added, 'There doesn't seem to be much about Him in those Old Testament Scriptures.' I feel sure I am not the only man who, as a new Christian, has thought that. So, when we read the Old Testament, we must try to see how it looks ahead. Chiefly, we must look for Christ in the Old Testament.

Second, we must look at Christ to know what facets of God's character are most important *for us*. Please note those two words, 'for us'. It would be absurd for mere man to analyse God's nature to point out what is of most and what is of least importance in it. That would be preposterous for two reasons:

1) It would imply an exhaustive knowledge of God, and

2) It would imply a division in God.

But we have no such knowledge of God, and God is indivisible. By all means, we must leave that subject alone.

But in the life and death and resurrection of Jesus Christ we may find what in God's character is most important for us to grasp. What God is, Christ is *for us*. Judah is told, 'Behold your God!' (Isaiah 40:9). But 'we preach . . . Christ Jesus the Lord' (2 Corinthians 4:5). Let us examine Christ. Let us see what parts of God's character are best seen in the Lord Jesus. Then let us major on those things. This will give us a biblical sense of proportion.

We must consider also the central place the cross takes in the New Testament. Somehow it is the wounded Christ – wounded to death – who is repeatedly held up before us. Here are Jesus' words:

> The Son of man came . . . to give his life a ransom for many (Mark 10:45).
>
> And I, if I be lifted up from the earth, will draw all men unto me. This he said [John adds], signifying what death he should die (John 12:32, 33).

Listen to Paul:

> But we preach Christ crucified (1 Corinthians 1:23).
>
> I determined not to know anything among you, save Jesus Christ, and him crucified (1 Corinthians 2:2).
>
> God forbid that I should glory, save in the cross of our Lord Jesus Christ, by whom the world is crucified unto me, and I unto the world (Galatians 6:14).

We might cite many more texts where the sacrificial death of Christ is shown to be central. Across the centuries nothing has changed. Satan and his fiends may seek to wear out the church, but they cannot succeed. The slain Lamb is with His people.

> The accuser of our brethren [Satan] is cast down, which accused them before our God day and night. And they overcame him by the blood of the Lamb . . . (Revelation 12:10, 11).

The blood – that is, the sacrificial death of Christ – makes all the difference.

## C

It is from the cross that we learn which aspects of the divine character God is most concerned to display. We must look at the cross. The New Testament forces us to that point. The Gospels major on the last week of the Lord Jesus' life, that week in which dying hangs as a backdrop behind all else. The corn of wheat must die. That is the message. And when we turn to the Epistles we see how they pick that up. They give us the meaning of the cross. From creation to the cross God revealed His character. But most of all, and best of all, He has shown it in Christ at the cross.

What do we see there? God revealed! We must remember that God is a person. He cannot be divided. Still, at the cross we are continually brought back to two things about God. At the cross we confront His love and His justice. What holds Jesus to the cross? Not the spikes! They bear His weight. But Jesus is well able to dispose of His enemies and their nails and their cross. Yet He will not. Why not? Love and justice hold Him there.

Paul explains the cross in terms of love and justice.

Note how he gives God's reasons for the cross in Romans 3:26. God sent Christ to His death that God 'might be just, and the justifier of him which believeth in Jesus'. God must do two things, Paul says. He must be *just*. That is the first thing. God's justice had to come into play. But He had determined also to be *justifier*. So, He had to find a way for His love to act as well as for His justice to be brought out. He loved us enough to make us right with Him. But He loved Himself too much to do it in any unjust way. Christ crucified is His solution of the problem of love and justice joined at the cross. God bruised His Son, even to the death, that He might be just, yet the Justifier of the people whom His Son died to save.

These same two things moved Christ Himself. It was not only the Father who thought in terms of love and justice. Jesus did so too. We see it, for instance, in Mark 10:45. There He speaks of giving His life as 'a ransom for many'. You perhaps know of the discussions that have gone on in church history about this phrase. At one time some thought that the ransom was paid to Satan. But there could have been nothing just about such a transaction, for Satan has no God-given rights over man. He is a usurper.

But when once we see that the ransom is paid to God, we see Jesus' death in the light in which Jesus saw it. It is an act of justice. Christ gives Himself in exchange for His own. To be 'a ransom' He gave Himself up to the justice of God.

From the point of view of the motives of the men who killed Him, the death of Christ was the grossest miscarriage of justice. They cared nothing for justice. They wanted to be rid of Him. He threatened their position with the Roman government. And for that God will judge them.

But God's motive was pure. He saw to it that justice was done in the death of Christ. He poured out upon His Son the wrath due to His people, for He was their substitute. God thereby carried out His plan and work of salvation.

'It pleased the Lord to bruise him' and to put Him to grief. None else could accomplish such a work. In this way God's love and justice met. 'Mercy and truth met together; righteousness and peace kissed each other' (Psalm 85:10).

### D

What this world needs is the knowledge of God. Throughout the first part of this book I have said that when a man knows God he finds that two things are true. First, he has a motive for telling others about God. The more a man knows about God the more he finds God worthy of being proclaimed. Then, second, the fact that the man knows God supplies that man with a good part of his message. Life's grandest privilege is to help others to learn to know God in all the glory of His character and His deeds.

In this chapter I have added a caution. We must not forget that God is best known in Jesus Christ. It is 'in the face of Jesus Christ' that men will find God as they will not, and could not, find Him elsewhere. Furthermore, God would have us look especially at the Lord Jesus in His death. The crowning point of God's revelation is the cross – the sacrificial death of Christ. Here we see, evidently, the things that God is most concerned that we see: God's love, and God's justice. These two things meet in the death of Christ.

And now, what shall we do? That is the question we face in the remainder of this book. If indeed we have learned all that we think we have learned, what then?

A friend once said to me, 'Anything is interesting if you know enough about it.' Over the years I have come to agree with him. The driest subject can be entertaining if we know its ins-and-outs. And therein lies our danger.

The knowledge of God is the deepest subject that can engage our attention. Have we begun to get hold of it? Every true Christian has begun to do so, and some much more than others. But we must not treat that knowledge simply as a source of delight. We must do something more. We must follow in the train of those who, knowing God, have proclaimed Him. Here is our task. Here is an additional delight. This knowledge, like all knowledge, is enjoyed best when it is shared. And this knowledge of God, like no other knowledge, will bring life and health to a sin-sick world. It is the glory of the Christian to tell out the glory of God. God made us for this. Let us arise and do it with all our might!

## 10: *God's Glory and Human Need*

Every once in a while I meet some friend who objects to the sort of thing I am doing in this book. 'That's all well and good,' he says, 'all this *talk* about God. But, frankly, I'm after something practical. We will have all eternity to learn theology. Why don't we get on with the business of living the Christian life. That's what it's all about, isn't it?'

Now in one way I quite agree with that friend. I applaud his emphasis on 'the business of living the Christian life'. That is indeed what Christianity is about. And 'missions' is a part of that life. I must never forget that, not even for an instant. Neither must you. But when I ask what the *first business* in the living of the Christian life is, the Scriptures give me unexpected answers.

If by 'first business' I mean first in the order of time, the Scripture tells me that I must trust Christ. I must depend on His action, not my own. That comes before all else. If, on the other hand, by 'first business' I mean my foremost business, first in the order of importance, I am told to

love the Lord thy God with all thy heart, and with all thy soul, and with all thy mind. This is the first and great commandment (Matthew 22:37, 38).

I have called these unexpected answers. Let me show you why.

These answers are not at all 'practical'. Please note that I put the word 'practical' in quotation marks. I think they are immensely practical. I might go a step further and say that they are the most practical of all answers. But very likely they are not quite what my friend had in mind. They are odd from that point of view. He was thinking of actions, and these verses speak of attitudes. He was thinking horizontally, of what we do with our fellow man. These Scriptures look at life vertically, at our stance towards Christ and God.

Men often forget that there is the closest connection between what they believe and how they act. That is why they get impatient with theology. That is why they want to get beyond doctrine. In one way they seem right. Certainly if our brains are filled with a theology that never works itself out into godly living, they have every right to shake their heads at us. And, of course, it will be our acts against which they react. They cannot see our doctrine. They can see the way we live.

But still, there is a direct line that runs from our doctrine to our actions, from what is in our minds to what is in our words and ways. The Lord Jesus put it this way:

> Out of the abundance of the heart the mouth speaketh. A good man out of the good treasure of the heart bringeth forth good things: and an evil man out of the evil treasure bringeth forth evil things (Matthew 12:34, 35).

And what is the heart? It is the inner man with its

thoughts and purposes and motives. It is good treasure, or evil treasure. But whichever it is, it cannot be hidden. The heart spills over into life. Thoughts of God, and of all else, erupt into acts. The filling of the heart with wise thoughts of God becomes the most important, the most practical, business in the world.

## A

Just now I have a hymnal open before me. A minute or two ago I went downstairs in my home to get this hymnal so that I might remind myself of something that happened recently. I was at church. In the pulpit was a well-known minister from the Philippines. His theme was the crying need of his people. He described their plight plainly but eloquently, for many of his countrymen know nothing of the saving power of Christ. All of us, I trust, were moved.

Then came the time to close the service. I remember how pleased I was at the closing hymn our pastor chose. But I could not remember the hymn. All I could recall was that there were two hymns on the page, and that both spoke of the importance of telling of Christ. Of course, every missionary hymn does that. But these hymns made another point. They made the point of this book. God and Christ are worthy to be proclaimed for who They are.

The hymn we sang was, 'Ye servants of God, your Master proclaim'. Immediately below it was, 'O for a thousand tongues to sing'. Both are by that prince of hymnwriters, Charles Wesley. And in my hymnal both are classified under 'Hymns of Worship'. They are hymns of worship indeed!

109

The thing that pleased me was this: the hymn we sang brought a needed balance to what we had heard. Yes, men are needy. And yes, they will perish without Christ. Let us never forget those truths. Let us emphasize them. But our danger, it seems to me, lies in another direction. It lies in forgetting God in our zeal for men. The two hymns I have mentioned are not simply hymns of praise. Praise is directed primarily to God. But these songs address men. In the first, Charles Wesley exhorts *us* to proclaim the glory of God and Christ. In the second, he exhorts *himself* to do the same! And he calls on his 'gracious Master' to help him 'spread through all the earth abroad the honours of Thy name'.

I fear this is a missing note in much of modern evangelicalism. I hope I realize how easy, how cheap, it is to say such a thing. But I believe it is so. I may use myself as an example of what I am decrying. Over the years I have given many missionary appeals. Yet to this day I find it easier to speak of men's needs than to speak of the privilege of making Christ known. And I say this as one who is well aware of how much the emphasis on Christ is needed. My head tells me what to do, but so often I fail to do it. Why? My sinfulness helps to explain the failure. But beyond that, I have to ask myself a question. How far am I a product of my Christian culture? How far am I moulded by our evangelical 'climate'?

Where are the missionary candidates who are panting to make Christ known *for Christ's sake*? Do they exist? They must exist, for these candidates are Christians. And surely a Christian wants his Saviour to be known. But yet the question returns. Why do we hear so little of this desire, and so much of the needs of men?

Perhaps you can better feel my concern if we look into the past. And the most important document of the past, on this matter, is the New Testament. What does *it* say? That is our first question.

**B**

The New Testament shows a great awareness of the needs of men. The Lord Jesus sets the example of compassion for the lost. He felt keenly the needs of the masses. He helped them in their physical need. He fed the five thousand. He fed the four thousand. Above all He helped them in their spiritual need. He taught the truth. He pointed to Himself as the way to God. Finally He died for needy men. All of this is true, and immensely important.

How surprised we are, then, to read the Great Commission! Each of the Gospels tells us that Jesus sends His servants into the world. The Book of Acts also tells how the Lord Jesus commissioned them. But these various accounts of what we call the 'Great Commission' say virtually nothing about what men need. Listen to the Lord Jesus speaking in Matthew:

> All power is given unto me in heaven and in earth. Go ye therefore, and teach all nations, baptizing them in the name of the Father, and of the Son, and of the Holy Ghost: teaching them to observe all things whatsoever I have commanded you: and, lo, I am with you alway, even unto the end of the world. Amen. (28:18–20).

It is not that the needs of men are unimportant. But this statement is made from another standpoint.

Listen to the Lord Jesus once more.

> Ye shall receive power after that the Holy Ghost is come upon you: and ye shall be witnesses unto me both in Jerusalem, and in all Judaea, and in Samaria, and unto the uttermost part of the earth (Acts 1:8).

Here again is the same standpoint.

How shall we describe these statements? They are kingly. They are royal. They show the Lord's consciousness of His own majesty and standing. We may see this in two ways.

1) The Lord *commands* His subjects. 'Go' is not optional. The King speaks. We must obey.

2) The commission is designed to create more subjects. 'Tell them who I am,' the Lord Christ says in effect. 'And tell them to submit themselves to Me! Tell them to do everything I have commanded you!' Luke alone mentions any benefits they may receive. In Luke 24:47 the Lord Jesus holds forth 'remission of sins'. In all the rest there is no mention of advantages to men at all. The King speaks. Let men listen! Men's needs are not unimportant. But they do not come first in the Lord's thinking.

In a moment I hope to take up how the Apostles reacted to these facts. We will see how they understood Jesus. But first I want to look at a possible objection. I can imagine someone saying: 'It is all well and good to play down the needs of men, but the fact is this. If men were not needy Christ would not have come. If men were not needy Jesus would not have died. If men were not needy, there would have been no 'Great

Commission'! So it still comes back to this. The need of mankind is the reason for it all. The need of men, then, is the chief motive for getting out the gospel. And it is the chief part of the message. We must tell men that Christ will meet their needs.'

It is not hard to imagine someone saying this. Some such thoughts as these must lie behind much that we hear today. Why else would there be such an emphasis on the needs of men in our missionary appeals? Why else would we hear so little of the greatness of Christ in these same appeals? Why do I myself have such difficulty in putting God and Christ first in my own missionary appeals? Is it because I myself have not grasped the very truth I am trying to teach others? Each of us must answer these questions for himself. May God help us!

But the objection misses one point. The needs of sinful men could not have been the *whole* story. Why? Because there need not have been any sinful men! God could have made a world in which no such men ever existed. Certainly we want to tread carefully here. We do not know all that God thought in allowing sin. Perhaps we do not know a millionth part. But we know one thing. Sin did not surprise God. The God who knows all has not learned anything. He knew all things before He made man. He foresaw the entrance of sin, and yet He made man.

If we ask 'why?' we must balance our ignorance against our knowledge. Here we will ask Paul to take us by the hand. I want to put his words in two columns. Both verses are taken from Romans, chapter eleven:

| *Our Ignorance* | *Our Knowledge* |
|---|---|
| O the depth of the riches both of the wisdom and knowledge of God! how unsearchable are his judgments, and his ways past finding out! (v. 33). | For of him, and through him, and to him, are all things: to whom be glory for ever. Amen (v. 36). |

In verse 33 Paul makes this point: how little we know! The ways of God are beyond us. We can not trace them out. We are but men!

Yet that is not all that Paul says. There are things we can know. We can know what God tells us. And God tells us, through Paul, that all things serve His purposes. All things are for His glory. Behind all else lies the glory of God. Always and everywhere, God is to shine forth. This is true in missions, as in all else. This is why God is forming His church. As Paul puts it again:

> Unto him be glory in the church by Christ Jesus throughout all ages, world without end. Amen. (Ephesians 3:21).

And once again:

> Whether therefore ye eat, or drink, or whatsoever ye do, do all to the glory of God (1 Corinthians 10:31).

Does this keep us from remembering the needs of men? Absolutely not! But it puts those needs in perspective. They are not first. Our first goal is ever and always the same. We seek to bring praise to God. That – above all else – is the purpose of missions!

The apostles, of course, were the first Christian missionaries. The Book of Acts tells us of their work. If what I have said is true, they will show it by the way they preach and teach. That should be an acid test. Let us look for their motives. Then let us look at what they said.

We have already seen the commission Christ gave these men. They were to tell about Him (see Acts 1:8). Did they understand that? Did they know what Christ wanted them to do? Yes, they did! Our first clue comes in that same first chapter of Acts. Peter says that some man must be found to take Judas' place. Why? Look at Peter's answer:

> Wherefore of these men which have companied with us . . . must one be ordained to be a witness with us of his resurrection (vv. 21, 22).

Peter knew that men were needy. But that is not what he talked about. Instead he mentions the resurrection. That is, he points to a fact about Christ. He is thinking in the same terms as the Lord Jesus did when He sent Peter and the others forth.

Peter's preaching in Acts 2 shows the same understanding. What did he preach about? God and Christ! He refers to his hearers in passing. He tells them that they are wrong in thinking that the disciples are drunk (v. 15). He reminds them of some things they knew (vv. 22, 29). And he points out his hearers' wickedness (v. 23). But these things are not the burden of this message. The message is Christ. Or – to enlarge – God and Christ and the Spirit. 'God,' says Peter in effect,

115

'sent Christ. Christ sent the Spirit. That is why you see and hear these things.'

Then Peter reaches the climax, and once again he mentions his hearers.

> Therefore let all the house of Israel know assuredly, that God hath made that same Jesus, whom ye have crucified, both Lord and Christ (v. 36).

It is not that his hearers were unimportant. Peter, no doubt, longed to help them. But something came before that concern. He had to tell of Christ. And his hearers were not to ask, 'What is there in it for me?' They had to know that Jesus is Lord. And they had to act accordingly! No wonder 'they were pricked in their heart'! (v. 37). No wonder they asked what they must do to be saved! They had not been told that God had sent His word to them to make them happy. They had been told that they stood before a King whom they had offended. This was God-centred preaching. Peter preached that God was worthy to be known and proclaimed for who He is.

And this note continues. Look at what Peter and John do when they are arrested in Acts 4. Their whole message is Jesus Christ. Listen to Peter:

> Ye rulers of the people, and elders of Israel. If we this day be examined of the good deed done to the impotent man, by what means he is made whole; be it known unto you all, and to all the people of Israel, that by the name of Jesus Christ of Nazareth, whom ye crucified, whom God raised from the dead, even by him doth this man stand here before you whole.
>
> This is the stone which was set at nought of you builders, which is become the head of the corner. Neither

is there salvation in any other: for there is none other name under heaven given among men, whereby we must be saved (vv. 8–12).

We read these words nineteen centuries later. They do not carry the sting to us that Peter intended. Take the word, 'salvation'. To us it suggests pleasant thoughts. To 'be saved' means to have all the benefits of the gospel.

But put yourself in the rulers' position. Then listen again. 'You set Jesus aside,' says Peter. 'You did it! How then can you be saved from the effect of what you have done? I will tell you. You must be saved by this same person. You must be saved by Jesus Christ!' Not a word here of peace and joy! They had offended God. They must be put right. And only Jesus Christ could do it!

Why do Peter and John speak in this way? When the rulers forbid them to preach they tell us:

> Whether it be right in the sight of God to hearken unto you more than unto God, judge ye. For we cannot but speak the things which we have seen and heard (vv. 19–20).

Here is their commission. They will carry it out. It comes before their own needs. They must tell what they have seen and heard of Christ. They dare not hesitate, whatever the cost. That is why they pray,

> And now, Lord, behold their threatenings: and grant unto thy servants, that with all boldness they may speak thy word' (v. 29).

They know their own weakness. And they pray to be protected from it. Nothing else matters. They must

117

boldly speak God's word. And what is that word? Luke tells us in verse 33:

> And with great power gave the apostles witness of the resurrection of the Lord Jesus.

When God answered their prayer they spoke of Christ. They knew that the people needed their message. But that was not their chief motive. Their whole bearing said, 'We are under orders!' The gospel was delivered to them. They had to pass it on. That was their first concern. They could have said what Paul said later:

> For though I preach the gospel, I have nothing to glory of: *for necessity is laid upon me: yea, woe is unto me, if I preach not the gospel!* (1 Corinthians 9:16).

They dare not neglect men, but God is their first reason for spreading the gospel. The God who is supremely worthy of being known has sent them.

### D

But I must also emphasize something else. When I say that God was the apostles' *first* reason for spreading the gospel I do not wish to be misunderstood. 'First' does not mean 'only'. There is a large difference here; I must not overlook it.

Is it possible to be God-centred and to ignore the needs of men? Certainly not! That must be the farthest thing from our minds. Let me give you two reasons for saying so.

First, to be God-centred means, in part, to think as God thinks. When He tells us, for instance, that His thoughts are not like our own we are not to rest content with that fact. As far as possible we are to adopt God's thoughts. When God says, 'Come now and let us reason together' on any subject, it is because He wishes to lead us to think as He does. Or, to use New Testament words, we are to have 'the mind of Christ'. Always – on everything – so far as that is humanly possible!

And what does God think of human need? Can any Christian doubt the answer? God is so intensely concerned for needy men that He has sent His Son to die for them. The heart of God towards poor, distressed sinners is fully unveiled at the cross. For us to be God-centred means to have this same compassionate heart!

We must also remember one other fact. The same God who has saved us and sent us to the lost has done more than that. He commanded us to love our neighbours as ourselves. And He has told us that we must not 'love in word, neither in tongue; but in deed and in truth' (1 John 3:18). The profession of love is easy. We all know that talk is cheap. But God Himself has set us the example we must follow. In John's words again:

> Herein is love, not that we loved God, but that he loved us, and sent his Son to be the propitiation for our sins (1 John 3:10)

God's love for men sent Christ to the cross. That is our example; that is our model. It is the example the apostles followed. Nothing that I have already said above is intended to deny that. When we have loved our neighours to the extent of dying to bring them the gospel we will have fulfilled our debt to them. Until then our duty is plain. Our hearts must long for, and cry over, the sinful burdens of dying men. And the longing and cry must be translated into action. Then, and only then, will our lives be fully God-centred.

# 11: *David Brainerd before God*

I told you when I started that I hoped to do two things. I hoped to show that God is worthy to be known and proclaimed for who He is. I did not expect you to deny that. But I hoped to put it before you in a way that you could not forget. That is what I have tried to do.

Now I come to the second thing. I want to motivate you; I want to move you. I have said that 'those who know the most about God are the most responsible and best equipped to tell of Him'. I urge you not to forget this truth. Just to the degree that you know God, just to that degree you must make Him known. God is still largely unknown in many parts of the earth. Does this leave you unmoved? Will *you*, who know more of God than many do, will *you* remain unconcerned? I believe not. I trust not. I hope not.

We hear much nowadays about the following of examples, and I write these last chapters with that in mind. Instead of repeatedly exhorting you (and myself) to make God known, I want to do something more. I have picked out certain missionaries who are well-known and have long been models among evangelicals. And I hope to show you what moved them. In each case the prime motive will be the same. These men knew God. And they sought to bring Him glory by making Him known. They were not indifferent to the need of men, but they had a supreme passion. It was to declare the glory of God.

**A**

As I write I have David Brainerd's diary open before me. Brainerd, as you probably know, was a missionary to the American Indians. He did not labour long. He died a young man. Yet his story is widely known. Preaching through an interpreter, he sought to bring the Indians of New Jersey and Pennsylvania to Christ. Despite the handicaps of ill-health, extreme loneliness, and frequent exposure to freezing temperatures, Brainerd did his work. And God was pleased to bless Brainerd. Many Indians came to Christ. Brainerd saw what many of us have never seen. Brainerd saw revival!

Brainerd's diary is a revealing volume. It shows us the man's human qualities. We often see him, for instance, despairing for being of any use to God. More than most men, he suffered from depression. Entries like these are not uncommon:

*Thursday, Oct. 20* [1743]. Had but little sense of divine things this day. Alas, that so much of my precious time is spent with so little of God! Those are tedious days, wherein I have no spirituality.

*Thursday, Jan. 5* [1744]. Had an humbling and pressing sense of my unworthiness. My sense of the badness of my own heart filled my soul with bitterness and anguish; which was ready to sink, as under the weight of a heavy burden.

*Friday, Feb. 10.* Was exceedingly oppressed, most of

the day, with shame, grief, and fear, under a sense of my past folly, as well as present barrenness and coldness.

If you knew nothing of Brainerd's depression, reading these entries could make you wonder what kind of man Brainerd was!

But David Brainerd was a man with a passion. He tells us what it was in an entry dated August 23rd [1743]:

> . . . In evening prayer God was pleased to draw near my soul, though very sinful and unworthy: was enabled to wrestle with God, and persevere in my requests for grace. I poured out my soul for all the world, friends and enemies. *My soul was concerned, not so much for souls as such, but rather for Christ's kingdom, that it might appear in the world, that God might be known to be God in the whole earth.* [Italics mine] . . . Let the truth of God appear, wherever it is; and God have the glory for ever. Amen.

Here are the great themes: the truth of God, the kingdom of Christ, and God Himself as the grand goal of all things. Brainerd prays for his friends and enemies. But this act of prayer rises out of a higher vision. God must be known, and not simply by name. God's name was well-known, even in the wilds of New Jersey. God must be known as GOD! To Brainerd that was the great thing. Even Christ's kingdom serves that end. Let God be known! To know God is the great essential. And to make him known was Brainerd's task. That is why he prayed for souls.

Brainerd himself knew God. This knowledge of God was his equipment for battle. It saved him, for instance, from any peevishness towards God in his afflictions. So long as the God of the Bible was his God, Brainerd could bear up under depression. In some ways his trials rank with those of Job. The diary's pages make heart-rending reading. But the glory of God is at their centre. The Indians, 'my people' as he loved to call them, are important. But nowhere do they compete with God. Let God be glorified! That is Brainerd's burden.

I want to trace this further. Look at these entries:

> *Friday, Oct. 5* [1744] . . . After some consultation, the Indians gathered, and I preached to them . . . I was exceedingly sensible of the impossibility of doing any thing for the poor heathen without special assistance from above: and my soul seemed to rest on God, and leave to him to do as he pleased in that which I saw was his own cause . . .
>
> *Thursday, Dec. 6* . . . towards night I felt my soul rejoice, that God is unchangeably happy and glorious; *that he will be glorified, whatever becomes of his creatures.* [Italics mine.]

And one final entry – an entry in which Brainerd dares to address the angels!

> *Tuesday, Feb. 7* [1744] . . . O ye angels, do ye glorify him incessantly; and if possible, prostrate yourselves lower before the blessed King of heaven? I long to bear a part with you; and, if it were possible, to help you. Oh, when we have done all that we can, to all eternity, we shall not be able to offer the ten thousandth part of the homage that the glorious God deserves!

Brainerd longed to help the angels tell out God's glory. No doubt he has had that wish granted! But when he wrote those words Brainerd was yet in the flesh. What could he do then? His desire was fulfilled, in part, by telling his poor Indians of God's greatness. He did not have the 'thousand tongues' for which, like Charles Wesley, he might have wished. Brainerd did not use even one tongue that the Indians could understand. An interpreter was his tongue to them. But with all his soul he set forth the glory of God as it is seen in Christ. May God help us to follow his example!

**B**

Do we share Brainerd's vision of God? I do not ask whether we always *feel* His glory. I know the answer. We do not! My question has to do with our conviction concerning God. Do we accept the propriety of Brainerd's words to the angels? Is he correct? Or are his words mere space fillers? Or, worse yet, are they a delusion? I do not think you will find it hard to answer these questions.

The world, however, does not have this vision. The people who have not heard cannot join the chorus of praise. How, then, can they do what the Psalmist commands them? Listen to him.

Make a joyful noise unto the Lord, all ye lands. Serve the Lord with gladness: come before his presence with singing. Know ye that the Lord he is God: it is he that hath made us, and not we ourselves; we are his people, and the sheep of his pasture.

Enter into his gates with thanksgiving, and into his courts with praise: be thankful unto him, and bless his name. For the Lord is good; his mercy is everlasting; and his truth endureth to all generations (Psalm 100).

Unlike many of the Psalms, this one is not first of all

addressed to Israel, but to 'all lands'. He means that the whole earth must praise the Lord. The earth must know that the Lord is God. And we cannot but admire his emphasis.

But how shall men know, and how shall they sing? The Psalm does not tell us, but other Scriptures make it plain. If they are to know the Lord, savingly, we must display His character. We must show His works. If they are to sing we must give them the song. If they 'enter into his gates with thanksgiving', they will enter with us. They will hear our song of praise. They will join our choir. Together we will 'make a joyful noise unto the Lord!'

Here again Brainerd is our example. He too longed to hear the heathen sing. And when God was pleased to save some of the Indians, Brainerd saw their conversion in that light. Now they would praise God. And now God's glory would be better known. Note these words taken from his diary:

> *Wednesday, June 4* [1746] . . . I could only rejoice, that God had done the work himself; and that none in heaven or earth might pretend to share the honour of it with him. I could only be glad, that God's declarative glory was advanced by the conversion of these souls . . . Oh that he might be adored and praised by all his intelligent creatures, to the utmost of their power and capacities! My soul would have rejoiced to see others praise him, though I could do nothing towards it myself.

How much this reads like words in 2 Corinthians, chapter four, where Paul tells us what drives him. In verse 11 he mentions his perils. They are 'for Jesus' sake'. But in verse 15 he expands his statement:

For all things are for your sakes, that the abundant grace might through the thanksgiving of many redound to the glory of God.

Does Paul labour for Jesus' sake or for his converts' sake? Clearly he toils for Jesus and for his converts alike. But equally clearly his final end, his grand goal, is the glory of God. Paul's converts join Paul in giving thanks to God. That is what Paul is after! That is why he does not faint (v. 16). That is why he sees his trials as 'light affliction' (v. 17). Paul's goal is to glorify God. And that goal is achieved as more and more men turn to God and give Him thanks!

## C

The goal of creation is that men might praise the Lord. Paul learned that lesson. So did Brainerd after him. Yet that will not fully account for their passion to make God known. One thing more was true. Paul and Brainerd knew God for themselves. They did not simply parrot the words, 'God must be praised'. They knew the utter worthiness of God, and proclaimed Him as 'God over all, blessed for ever'. That moved them. That drove them forward. They knew that the man who knows the most about God is best equipped and most responsible to tell of Him. They knew that they knew Him. And what they knew seemed so good that it had to be spread far and wide. No wonder their converts praised God. The converts had been shown the grand and glorious God.

But Paul and Brainerd are not an exclusive company. We must join them. They teach us that anything we

127

have learned of God's glory we have the duty to share. It is not enough to aim to save men from hell. We must aim to save them *for* something. We must show them the majesty of our God. We cannot but long to hear them join the chorus of praise. We must say with the Psalmist:

> Oh that men would praise the Lord for his goodness, and for his wonderful works to the children of men! (Psalm 107:8, 15, 21, 31!)

Our world is larger than it was in Paul's day. It is larger than it was in Brainerd's. Paul knew nothing of much of the world's area. David Brainerd knew but little of its lost tribes. Each of their worlds was much smaller than our own. There are many more people in this world to praise God than they dreamed of. Yet God has not changed. He is as worthy of our praise as ever!

Our larger world must not discourage us. It calls us to greater effort. There is a great God to be known. There is a great world to know Him! We must tell them and call forth their praise. If the task seems overwhelming let us pray the prayer of the Psalmist:

> God be merciful unto us, and bless us; and cause his face to shine upon us (Psalm 67:1).

Why? So that we may simply sun ourselves in His goodness? Not at all! Listen further.

> That thy way may be known upon earth, thy saving health among all nations (v. 2).

And why should God's way be known? Here is the Psalmist's answer:

> Let the people praise thee, O God; let all the people

praise thee. O let the nations be glad and sing for joy: for thou shalt judge the people righteously, and govern the nations upon earth (vv. 3, 4).

God's way must be known so that God will be known. And when God is known as He is, one thing must follow. People will praise Him! The nations will be glad and sing for joy when they become His peoples. His government will not be a burden to them. Instead they will sing God's praise. They will abound in glory to God!

## 12: *Another Look at William Carey*

The last chapter closed with some verses from the Psalms. They were a prayer. The Psalmist cried for mercy. He asked for God's blessing. And he had a reason that lay outside himself. He wanted the heathen to learn God's way and give praise to the Lord. I suggested that his prayer should be our prayer too.

In one way a call to prayer is an odd thing. It sounds to some like a substitute for action. I hope that no one will suppose that prayer can replace the preaching of the gospel. It cannot; that is not its purpose.

But consider this. We profess to believe that all is vain without the Spirit of God. Do we believe that? If so, we shall start with prayer. If we do not ask for God's presence in our labours we should not be surprised if He does not work. If we do not ask for His wisdom we show ourselves to be fools. Yes, we must have prayer, and we must have it first. We must ask the Lord to glorify Himself to the ends of the earth.

**A**

Sometime in the mid-1780's a small association of Baptist churches in the midlands of England held their usual meeting. Out of it came an urgent request. The request was for prayer meetings to be held in each local church.

What prompted this request? The call to prayer gives the answer. These men thought that prayer was needed

> . . . to bewail the low state of religion, and earnestly implore a revival of their churches and of the general cause of the Redeemer, and for that end to wrestle with God for the effusion of His Holy Spirit.

It is not hard to sympathize with these requests. We could easily make them our own. But there was more. The call goes on:

> Let the whole interest of the Redeemer be affectionately remembered, and the spread of the Gospel to the most distant parts of the habitable globe be the objects of your most fervent requests.

A modern Christian is likely to find the quaint language the most striking thing about this call. We are used to appeals for prayer for missions. They reach us frequently. We do not live in the eighteenth century.

How different were things then? Think of this, for instance. It seems likely that none of the men who sent out this call had ever met what we would call 'a missionary'. Yes, there were missionaries then. But they were few in number. They were widely scattered, and they tended to stay in their fields of labour. Transportation was an enormous obstacle. If you went far from home you went to stay.

Nor was that all. These Baptist churches were then faced with a graver difficulty. They had largely fallen asleep under the influence of a false, pseudo-Calvinism.

Let one of their own ministers describe their problem. Here are his words:

> I found my soul drawn out in love to poor souls while reading Millar's account of Elliott's labours among the North American Indians, and their effect on those poor barbarous savages. I found also a suspicion that we shackle ourselves too much in our addresses; that we have bewildered and lost ourselves by taking the decrees of God as rules of action. Surely Peter and Paul never felt such scruples in their addresses as we do. They addressed their hearers as *men* – fallen men; as we should warn and admonish persons who were blind and on the brink of some dreadful precipice. Their work seemed plain before them. O that mine might be so before me!

The writer, Andrew Fuller, struggled in his soul. He knew well enough that God had not chosen (decreed) to save all men. He knew that God would pass some by. Here he was on scriptural ground. But the church around him was drawing awful consequences from this fact. Put plainly it was this: if our hearers are not among God's elect they are not bound to believe. And this: if they need not believe we need not preach to them. Sinners and saints could be left to slumber on!

Yet God was gracious to Andrew Fuller. He was beginning to see light ahead. Note these words: 'We have bewildered and lost ourselves by taking the decrees of God as rules of action.' Here is the heart of the matter: not God's decrees, but God's commands, are the Christian's rule!

In 1784 Fuller published a book that shook a larger circle than his own. In *The Gospel Worthy Of All Acceptation* he opens with two propositions that seem self-evident to us.

1) Unconverted sinners are commanded to believe in Christ.

[Then he moves to a broader principle.]

2) Every man is bound cordially to receive what God reveals.

Fuller is out in the sunlight, and his friends are rapidly following him. No wonder they cry out to God for revival and 'the general cause of the Redeemer'!

The call to prayer, however, goes beyond this. It looks at a fallen world, and it sees no boundaries until the ends of the earth are reached. Clearly the little group is being led to see further than it first dreamed possible. One grand truth points to another. And all of them require prayer to God for wisdom and blessing.

## B

About this time young William Carey came to Moulton, Northamptonshire. He began to preach, and he entered into the same fellowship of ministers. James Culross, a 19th-century biographer of Carey, tells how Carey reacted to Fuller's book.

> Carey said to him: 'If it be the duty of all men, where the gospel comes, to believe unto salvation, then it is the duty of those entrusted with the gospel to endeavour to make it known among the nations for the obedience of faith.' The one thing seemed to him a corollary to the other.

And so it seems to us. Yet, to many, the thought smacked of novelty.

At first, Carey's minister friends were unable to follow him. They had called for prayer for 'the spread of the Gospel to the most distant parts of the habitable globe'. God had brought them that far. And the Lord was about to answer their prayer, yet they were not ready for the answer!

An oft-repeated story well illustrates Carey's difficulties. In a meeting of the ministers he offered a topic for discussion. He thought they should discuss

> whether the command given to the apostles to teach all nations was not binding on all succeeding ministers to the end of the world, seeing that the accompanying promise was of equal extent.

Carey read the Lord's promise to be with His church to the 'end of the world (age)'. That seemed to settle it. Christ's promise went with Christ's command. Both were for the whole age. It would not be right to claim the one without the other. Such was Carey's vision. And surely Carey was right.

But the story goes on. No sooner had Carey offered this topic than it was rudely swept aside. 'Young man, sit down, sit down,' he was told. 'You are an enthusiast. When God pleases to convert the heathen, He will do it without consulting you or me.'

The exact details of the story are doubtful. Whether John Ryland, Sr. (the man who is supposed to have said these things) ever said them is debatable. But it is clear that Carey was rebuked for bringing up the subject. And, for the moment, he had to let it drop.

In our pride we must not judge these men too harshly. We are too ready to do so. Instead, we must try to understand them. Here is the hopeful side to their story:

1) The prayed; they believed in prayer; and their belief passed into action.

2) They clung tenaciously to God's sovereignty. They believed that God disposed of His workers and His work as He pleased.

In both these things these men are models for us. And Carey was with them. It was not a case of Carey being on one side and his minister friends on the other. They were at one on these two truths. To the end of his life Carey clung to God's sovereignty as tenaciously as any! In fact, that very sovereignty of God encouraged him to press on with his labours.

Let us listen in as William Carey writes to Fuller from India in 1812. The letter brings dreary news. The printing plant has been burned to the ground. Precious manuscripts, the work of years, by Carey himself, have gone up in smoke. Carey continues:

> The ground must be laboured over again, but we are not discouraged . . . We have all been supported under the affliction, and preserved from discouragement. To me the consideration of the divine sovereignty and wisdom has been very supporting . . . I endeavoured to improve this our affliction last Lord's-day, from Psalm xlvi. 10, 'Be still and know that I am God.' I principally dwelt upon two ideas, viz.:
>
> 1. God has a sovereign right to dispose of us as he pleases.
> 2. We ought to acquiesce in all that God does with us and to us.

'What God does to us!' Could God's sovereignty be better expressed than it is in those five words? Not a word about Satan. Nothing about suspected arsonists.

135

Not a syllable about 'accidents' or 'bad luck'. No! – this affliction is something 'God has done to us'.

To Carey God's sovereignty was meat and drink. Many today can hardly understand this. The reason is not hard to find. There is confusion over the meaning of God's sovereignty. One might ask: Does not every Christian believe in the sovereignty of God? Most Christians profess such a belief. But so often that 'sovereignty' turns out to be God's bare *right* to rule. There is no firm conviction that God exercises that right. 'Free will' and other obstacles are thought to limit Him. No such limits were felt by Carey and his friends.

And this explains their call to prayer. Motives for prayer vary. To these men there was one compelling reason to pray for 'the ends of the earth'. They fully believed that the whole process of world evangelization was in God's hands. He would choose the time. He would choose the workers. He would choose the places of ministry. What could be more necessary, then, than to pray! May God give us grace to follow them!

C

This question of prayer for missions demands a further look. We must not tip our hats to it and go on to 'important things'. Let us stay here a while.

The teaching in Scripture is that God's glory is the great end of creation. God has made all things to bring Him praise. That is why He has made us. God makes even man's wrath to praise Him (Psalm 76:10). All things bring Him glory.

Yet we must say more. It is one thing to bring God

glory; it is another thing to *aim* at His glory. In the task of missions we *aim* to bring God praise, to see God glorified.

God has told us how to bring Him glory. He has told us to do it by asking *Him* to do it. Do we hope to bring God glory? Then our first act must be a prayer, summed up in the words, 'Hallowed be thy name.' That is where Jesus started in giving us the model prayer. That is where we must start. If God is to be praised in the ends of the earth God must bring it about. Can we have a part? Yes, we can. But our part starts with this prayer, 'O God, magnify yourself! Lord, bring praise to your name!' That is what the Lord Jesus is teaching us. We must not miss His point.

Nor is that all. Jesus went further. He commanded prayer for the specific work of missions. Mission work involves the sending forth of workers. It cannot be done simply by praying. Men must go forth. Labourers are needed. Where shall they come from? Who will send them out? Jesus taught us to tackle these 'practical' problems by prayer.

> But when [Jesus] saw the multitudes, he was moved with compassion on them, because they fainted, and were scattered abroad, as sheep having no shepherd. Then saith he unto his disciples, The harvest truly is plenteous, but the labourers are few; pray ye therefore the Lord of the harvest, that he will send forth labourers into his harvest. (Matthew 9:36–38)

Look closely at these words. But first, I want us to avoid the temptation to treat these words as a mere introduction to chapter 10 of Matthew's Gospel. Let me explain what I mean.

Over the years I have heard many sermons on this passage. Often they have had this in common, that the real object of the sermon was to urge us to go to the mission fields. With that in mind the speaker would point out what happened in chapter 10 where the Lord Jesus sends forth His apostles as missionaries to Israel. The object lesson was something like this: 'It is not enough to pray. We must answer our own prayers. We must go forth. That is what the twelve did. That is what we must do.'

Do not misunderstand me. This book is written to appeal for workers for missions. But that does not give us licence to misuse Scripture. If we treat the passage I have quoted as a mere introduction to chapter 10 we are likely to miss its point. The point is this: prayer is our first work in the harvest. And the reason is not hard to find. It is this: the harvest has a 'Lord'. He oversees the harvest. Someone supplies the workers. Someone controls the progress. And that 'Someone' is God. Our first business is not to look at the size of the harvest. Our first business is to pray to our God.

In this, as in much else, Jesus is our example. In Psalm 2 Christ tells us how He was made King.

> I will declare the decree [He says]: the Lord hath said unto me, Thou art my Son; this day have I begotten thee. (v. 7)

The 'begetting' in this verse is not connected with birth, but, as verse 6 shows, with kingship.

Now, what does Christ do as King? Here is what God the Father tells Him to do:

> Ask of me, and I shall give thee the heathen for thine

inheritance, and the uttermost parts of the earth for thy possession. (v. 8)

His first work as King is to pray! Yes, He shall do much more than that. But that comes first. 'Ask of me!' says God. 'The harvest is in My hands. There will be no harvest without asking Me!'

It goes without saying that Christ did thus 'ask'. We would know that, even if we had no direct evidence of it. He came to do God's will. And He did it! But in John's Gospel, chapter 17, the Scripture enables us to see Christ at prayer. And what do we find? We find Him preparing to enter into His kingship.

> Father [He prays], the hour is come; glorify thy Son, that thy Son also may glorify thee. (v. 1)

The hour of His exaltation has arrived. He is about to sit down in His Father's throne. He will be King indeed.

But that is not all. As Christ goes on praying, His words show His dependence on His Father. He has entered into the spirit of the phrase, 'Ask of Me!' He knows from where His followers have come. He calls them 'the men which thou gavest me out of the world'. We cannot doubt that He asked for them. And God has answered His prayer!

Two things are plain, then. First, Christ commands us to pray to his Father (Matthew 9:38). The command teaches us our dependence on God. We can do nothing alone. Success is in His hands.

Second, we have Christ's example. He was King, but He prayed as a dependent child. He sought God's glory through the conversion of men. He does that

139

still. But He does not do it alone. He looks to God the Father. He intercedes for men. His hope of success, like ours, rests in the hand and will of God. The Son of God prays. How much more should we!

All this shows us what sort of workers are needed. *Those who know the most about God.* Perhaps it is presumptuous for any man to think he fits into that category. But this much is clear. A first qualification is belief in prayer. If our attitude is, 'Let us get to work at once!', we are suspect. The man who knows the greatness and glory of God cannot say that *first.* Later he can and must say it. But if he knows God his way is plain before him. He must pray, 'Father, glorify yourself. Father, send forth your workers.'

William Carey and his circle of friends are our models here. They prayed before they did anything else. Later they did much more. And so must we. But they knew their God, and they knew that the harvest was in His hands. Because they knew God they entered into the spirit of this saying: You can do more than pray after you have prayed; but you cannot do more than pray until you have prayed!

Can there be a greater preparation for a missionary than this? I think not. A missionary is a man who knows that the harvest is in the hands of God. If you know *that* you do not know everything. But you know something of God. And God is the message and motive of missions!

# 13: *The Example of Henry Martyn*

I want to use one more man to exhibit the spirit of the missionary. Here are words from his *Journal*, written January 13, 1804:

> How is my soul constrained to adore the sovereign mercy of God, who began His work in my proud heart, and carried it on through snares which have ruined thousands – namely, human learning and honours: and now my soul, dost thou not esteem all things but dung and dross, compared with the excellency of the knowledge of Christ Jesus my Lord? Yea, did not gratitude constrain me, did not duty and fear of destruction, yet surely the excellency of the service of Christ would constrain me to lay down ten thousand lives in the prosecution of it.

The writer of these words was Henry Martyn. In 1804 Martyn was not yet a missionary. He was a young man. He did not know how brief his life was to be. He did not know what life would hold. These were things he could not know.

There were, however, some things Martyn did know. He knew that he hoped to serve Christ. And he knew why he wanted to serve Him. The knowledge of Christ was excellent. Martyn saw that Christ was worthy to be known and served for who He is.

**A**

Henry Martyn was born in 1781, the third of four children. His mother was not a woman of robust health. She appears to have passed her poor health on to her children. When Henry died at the young age of thirty-one, he was the last of his family. His two sisters and his brother were already dead.

What Martyn lacked in physical strength he made up for in scholarship. And in pride! Here is his own picture of himself at eighteen. He was visiting his father. His father was about to die though Henry did not know it.

> The consummate selfishness and exquisite irritability of my mind were displayed in rage, malice, and envy, in pride and vain-glory and contempt of all; in the harshest language to my sister, and even to my father, if he happened to differ from my mind and will.

This is not a promising picture!

But then came 'the sovereign mercy of God'. The year was 1800. Martyn's teacher was the New Testament. Here he tells his sister what happened:

> I began to attend more diligently to the words of our Saviour in the New Testament, and to devour them with delight. When the offers of mercy and forgiveness were made so freely, I supplicated to be made partaker of the covenant of grace with eagerness and hope, and thanks be to the ever-blessed Trinity for not leaving me without comfort.

Henry Martyn was a new man in Christ!

At this point Henry Martyn had a year of study at Cambridge left. It was a good year. His devotion to Christ grew. In January, 1801, he came out Senior Wrangler (i.e. top mathematician) in a group of gifted men. But scholarship for self-glory had lost its charm. In its place was a burning desire to use his gifts for Christ. That flame grew till Henry Martyn found himself sailing for India to serve his Master.

In India Martyn threw himself into language study. His goal was Bible translation. He worked at Arabic, Persian, and Hindustani. By 1811 he had translated the New Testament into Hindustani. With this work behind him he set out for Arabia and Persia. Those lands would also have to have the New Testament in their own tongues. And Henry Martyn appeared to be the man to do the job!

**B**

So far I have drawn Martyn's life with broad strokes, making it read almost like one triumph after another. Victor in scholarship! Conqueror at translation! Fair-haired child of heaven! The list could go on. But we would search it in vain for any help for poor men like ourselves.

What we need to know of Henry Martyn has hardly yet appeared. It is not these things, primarily, which have endeared Martyn to generations of Christians. It is something else.

Henry Martyn was learning *to live on God*. In this he was like David Brainerd. Both men were greatly used. But that is not why we remember them. We turn to their lives for this other ingredient, *living on God*. Let me explain.

A man lives on God when he finds his inspiration,

143

not in his successes, but in the character of the One he serves. This is what the *Westminster Shorter Catechism* wants us to see in its first question.

Q. 1. *What is the chief end of man?*
A.  Man's chief end is to glorify God, and to enjoy him for ever.

I am interested here in that last phrase. What does it mean 'to enjoy him for ever'? I can enjoy myself. I can enjoy other men. But can I enjoy God? The framers of the Catechism were sure that believers could, and that they would 'for ever'! The Psalmist thought so too.

> Whom have I in heaven but thee? and there is none upon earth that I desire beside thee. My flesh and my heart faileth: but God is the strength of my heart, and my portion for ever. (Psalm 73:25, 26)

The New Testament also bears this out. Listen to this prayer of the Lord Jesus Christ:

> Father, I will that they also, whom thou hast given me, be with me where I am; that they may behold my glory, which thou hast given me: for thou lovedst me before the foundation of the world. (John 17:24)

What shall we do in eternity? Here is the Lord's answer. We shall behold His glory. Nor is that incidental. Not at all! Rather Jesus gives it as the reason why we should be there. And what is His 'glory'? It is what He is. In Christ God has drawn us the picture of His own character. Jesus reveals God. Is God glorious! Jesus Christ is God's answer. And we shall see and feel and enjoy and marvel at that answer for ever!

But back to Henry Martyn! I have said that he lived on God. What is the evidence for that statement?

Take this fragment from his journal. He wrote it on shipboard, February 13, 1806. He was sailing for India. He was ill. He was also sailing away from the woman that he loved, Lydia Grenfell. He would never see her again:

> I endeavoured to realise again the truth, that suffering was my appointed portion. . . . Yet after all, I was ready to cry out, What an unfortunate creature I am, the child of sorrow and care; from my infancy I have met with nothing but contradiction, but I always solaced myself that one day it would be better, and I should find myself comfortably settled in the enjoyment of domestic pleasures, whereas, after all the wearying labours of school and college, I am at last cut off from all my friends, and comforts, and dearest hopes, without being permitted even to hope for them any more.

Try to picture Martyn as he writes these things. What do you see? A man eaten with frustration? Let us hear him out:

> As I walked the deck, I found that the conversation of others, and my own gloomy surmises of my future trials, affected me far less with vexation than they formerly did, merely from this, that I took it as my portion from God, all whose dispensations I am bound to consider and receive as the fruits of infinite wisdom and love towards me. I felt, therefore, very quiet, and was manifestly strengthened from above with might in my inner man; therefore without any joy, without any pleasant considerations to balance my present sickness and gloom. I was contented from the reflection, that it was God who did it.

Here the romance is gone. Here the triumph is of a different kind. But it is real none the less. Let us try to understand it.

Take Martyn's last words first. 'It was God who did it.' In themselves there is no comfort in these words. None at all. If you do not believe me, try them on a friend. Look for some neighbour who knows nothing of the character of God. Wait till he suffers some great loss. Then tell him, 'It was God who did it.' Will he thank you for your words? I do not think so. He may believe you – even that is doubtful – but he will not thank you. He finds no comfort in those words.

Here is another phrase: 'I took it as my portion from God.' How much comfort is in those words? None at all, for many men! They say the same thing, 'God did it.' And that is no help to them in any way.

Henry's comfort was not in the word 'God'. It was in the character of God. And it was in the fact that Henry Martyn understood something of God's nature. His situation was gloomy, his hopes had been dashed, the sea was a peril, and he was ill. How did Henry receive these facts? 'I am bound to consider and receive [all these things] as the fruits of *infinite wisdom and love towards me*.' There is his answer! It is the only answer that will do. God is infinitely wise and loving. Here is a God worthy to be served for who He is. Henry Martyn lived on this God.

C

But let us move on. I want to show you how Martyn's knowledge of God affected his service. I have said that *those who know the most about God are the most responsible and best equipped to tell of Him*. Henry Martyn's life will illustrate the claim.

Martyn arrived in Calcutta on May 16, 1806.

146

Immediately a trial faced him. He had hoped to be sent into the interior where he would have more contact with the natives. At first it seemed that hope was vain. His fellow-workers wanted him in Calcutta. In his *Journal* for May 17th he wrestles with this:

> I have a great many reasons for not liking this; I almost think that to be prevented going among the heathen as a missionary would break my heart. Whether it be self-will or aught else, I cannot yet rightly ascertain. At all events I must learn submission to everything . . . I have forgotten that [God] ordereth everything. I have been bearing the burden of my cares myself, instead of casting them all upon Him.

You will see that Henry sought peace here by thinking on the sovereignty of God. But what effect did that have upon him? Did it remove his sense of responsibility? Here is his answer:

> I feel pressed in spirit to do something for God. Everybody is diligent, but I am idle; all employed in their proper work, but I tossed in uncertainty; I want nothing but grace; I want to be perfectly holy, and to save myself and those that hear me. I have hitherto lived to little purpose, more like a clod than a servant of God; now let me burn out for God.

Here is the answer from his own heart: *let me burn out for God!* Henry Martyn knew God. I have said that Henry Martyn lived on God. With what result? That knowledge bore fruit. It taught him his responsibility, and he never forgot the lesson. Here he is our model. Time spent thinking on God's character is never wasted. But it must not keep us back from the work.

We must burn inwardly at the thought of God's glory. Then we must burn out in service for God.

But there is something else. What of Martyn's equipment? Did his knowledge of God fit him for his task?

A sceptic might answer this question by pointing to Martyn's poor health. 'There's your effect,' he might say, 'of thinking too much about God!' It is true that Martyn did not spare himself, and he paid the price in an early death. But loving one's earthly life is not a main ingredient in missionary service.

What is the equipment a missionary needs? Many things, no doubt! Let me choose a few. Then let us see whether the knowledge of God helped Martyn attain them.

I think, first, of humility. How was it with this young man? Did the knowledge of God beat back his pride? Again his Journal will help us. It tells of two experiences on the same day (July 6, 1806). Either of them might have harmed a lesser man. The first has to do with the way he was received in Calcutta:

> Mr Limerick preached from 2 Peter 1:13, and spoke with sufficient plainness against me and my doctrines. Called them inconsistent, extravagant, and absurd. He drew a vast variety of false inferences from the doctrines, and thence argued against the doctrines themselves. To say that repentance is the gift of God was to induce men to sit still and wait for God. To teach that Nature was wholly corrupt was to lead men to despair; that men thinking the righteousness of Christ sufficient to justify, will account it unnecessary to have any of their own: this last assertion moved me considerably, and I started at hearing such downright heresy.

It is not hard to imagine Martyn's feelings at listening to this sermon. But Mr Limerick spoke on:

> He spoke of me as one of those who understand neither what they say nor whereof they affirm, and as speaking only to gratify self-sufficiency, pride and uncharitableness.

How did Martyn react to this? Not as an angel, to be sure! He felt the sting of it. Yet there was more. Listen to his words:

> I rejoiced at having the sacrament of the Lord's Supper afterwards, as the solemnities of that blessed ordinance sweetly tended to soothe the asperities and dissipate the contempt that was rising: and I think I administered the cup to . . . and . . . with sincere goodwill.

May God grant us all the wisdom to hear abuse of ourselves with as much grace as Martyn showed here! As he served the Lord's Table he thought of what Christ did for sinners, and his ire subsided.

Later that day something else tested his humility. He caught a glimpse of success.

> At night I preached on John iv.10, at the mission church, and, blessed be God!, with an enlarged heart. I saw . . . in tears, and that encouraged me to hope that perhaps some were savingly affected, but I feel no desire except that my God be glorified.

Then he adds this significant line:

> If any are awakened at hearing me, let me not hear of it if I should glory.

Here we see the direct effect of knowing God. God must be glorified. He must not be robbed of an ounce of the credit for awakening a soul. The greatness of God shows the instrument his nothingness. May God give us such humility!

Now what else does a missionary need? He needs hope. And, closely related, he needs patience. Will a knowledge of God produce these things? How will it be with this man who lives on God? Let us look again at Martyn's Journal. He writes in Dinapore where he was sent late in 1806. The entry is dated December 2, 1806:

> Mr F.'s conversation with me about the natives was again a great trial to my spirit; but in the multitude of my troubled thoughts I still saw that there is a strong consolation in the hope set before us. Let men do their worst, let me be torn to pieces, and my dear L. [Lydia Grenfell] torn from me; or let me labour for fifty years amidst scorn, and never seeing one soul converted; still it shall not be worse for my soul in eternity, nor worse for it in time. Though the heathen rage and the English people imagine a vain thing, the Lord Jesus, who controls all events, is my friend, my master, my God, my all . . . Oh, let me for a little moment labour and suffer reproach!

This entry speaks for itself. Here is patience doing its 'perfect work' (James 1:4). Here too is hope. Both are based on the knowledge of Christ. Christ 'controls all events'. That was more than enough.

The hope, however, in the above entry appears to be a hope for eternity. What of hope for the gospel's success in this world? Would the natives be converted? Or was Mr F. right in thinking it impossible? Note how God's character gives Martyn his answer in the next entry. The date is April 6, 1807.

'Our countrymen, when speaking of the natives, said, as they usually do, that they cannot be converted, and if they could they would be worse than they are. . . . It is surprising how positively they are apt to speak on this subject, from their never acknowledging God in anything: "Thy judgments are far above out of his sight." If we labour to the end of our days without seeing one convert, it shall not be worse for us in time, and our reward is the same in eternity. The cause in which we are engaged is the cause of mercy and truth, and therefore, in spite of seeming impossibilities, it must eventually prevail.'

In this entry, too, eternity is in sight. But there is also the kind of hope that God expects us to cherish. Not a hope in ourselves! We have too much of that; we think that God's work lives and dies with us. But that is reckoning without God. 'The cause of mercy and truth' is the cause of God. It is just as frail as God is. That is to say, it is not fragile at all!

There is one thing more the missionary needs. He needs a message. All else is vain without a message. The missionary must speak for God. So it is right to ask, 'How did Martyn's knowledge of God affect his message?'

It cannot be doubted that he preached the gospel in its broad outlines. His whole life was given to this. But let me show you something else. Notice the application Henry makes because he knows the God he serves. Among his letters is one to a Mrs Dare. The subject is a colonel with whom they were both acquainted.

He has, you know, all that heart can wish of this world's goods, and yet he is restless; sometimes the society is dull; at other times the blame is laid on the quarters, and he must go out of the cantonments. Today he is going

151

to Gya, to-morrow on the river. Now I tell him that he need not change his place, but his heart. Let him seek his happiness in God, and he will carry about a paradise in his own bosom.

'Let him seek his happiness in God.' There is a message for the world!

The God who is worthy to be known and served for who He is, is Himself the answer to this world's longings. And those who know Him best are best equipped to serve Him. He is their message. If we have discovered the glory of God in the face of Christ, we must not hold back. The God of glory must be made known. Have we learned to live on God? If we have, to any degree, we are equipped to that extent. We are equipped to serve the glorious God!

# 14: *Summing Up*

Nothing is easier than to criticize modern evangelicalism for low views of God. But the criticism is also a call. It calls us in two ways. First, it reminds us to deepen our own knowledge of God. 'Search the Scriptures,' Jesus said. 'They testify of me.' Do we want to learn of God and Christ? The Bible is our source. To mine its treasures is our life's work. Our goal is to find our satisfaction in God. May God help us to do so! The words of an early supporter of modern missions are helpful. His name was Samuel Pearce:

> It has pleased God lately to teach me more than ever that HIMSELF is the *fountain* of happiness; that likeness to him, friendship for him, and communion with him, form the basis of all true *enjoyment*. The very disposition which, blessed be my dear Redeemer! he has given me, to be anything, do anything, or endure anything, so that his name might be glorified, – I say, the *disposition* itself is heaven begun below.

Here we see the first part of that call being answered. And here we see that God Himself creates the disposition, the inclination, in our hearts.

This call, however, has another part. It reminds us of our responsibility, for we have some good treasure

153

that others need. We have the knowledge of God as He has made Himself known in Jesus Christ. If low views of God will not save this world – and they will not – then our task is clear. We must pray that God will send His messengers (and ourselves if He chooses to send us) to the ends of the earth with the message of God in Christ. How easy it is to criticize! How readily we may point the finger at others! What little effort it costs! And how little it will accomplish!

If there is a speck in our brother's eye, the Lord Jesus tells us, it deserves attention. Let us help our brother. But there is something we must do first. We must remove the rafter in our own eye. Can it be that we who claim to know God best have turned a blind eye toward a dying world? Could that *possibly* happen?

Captain James Cook was a South Seas explorer. God allowed him to make great discoveries. To some of my readers Cook's name may be a household word. How many of us know that he speculated about missions to the islands he discovered? Would missionaries *ever* visit them? Here is his answer:

> It is very unlikely that any measure of this kind should ever be seriously thought of, as it can neither serve the purpose of public ambition nor private avarice; and, without such inducements, I may pronounce that it will never be undertaken.

Obviously Cook here reckons without God. The prophecies of all men who do so must surely fail. James Cook, however, understood human nature. He knew something of the ambition and avarice that move and prevail with men. There you have this world's motives. And a sea captain would know them well!

God has lifted the eyes of His church higher than Cook could imagine. He has shown us a lost world, and He has taught us compassion. We have seen it in the face of Jesus Christ. It has moved us. The sight of lost men has called the church to the ends of the earth. A godly appeal has gone out: save those yet mired in heathen darkness! That is a great appeal. With shame we must confess that we have sometimes heard it with indifference. But the church at large has often responded. Thank God for that!

But there is still more to do, and there is greater reason for doing it. So often the vision of the changeless glory of God has been lost in our appeals. Is God less glorious than in Paul's day? Is He less majestic than in Carey's time? Has Christ lost His kingship since India was first evangelized? Does the Sovereign Lord of 1800 now wring His hands at His inability to send and to succeed? Surely not! Yet one might think so in hearing certain of our modern missionary appeals.

What, then, must we do? We must take up Paul's words, 'forgetting those things which are behind'. We need not look back. We must push ahead. We must tell out God's glory among the nations. Do not misunderstand me. I have no desire to deny our indebtedness to a lost world. I cannot afford to do without the compassion that must move a Christian heart. But these great motives are not at odds with one another. Not at all!

On May 24, 1810, William Carey wrote these words:

It is now nearly seventeen years since I left England for this country [India]. Since that time I have been witness to an astonishing train of circumstances, which have produced a new appearance of all things relating to the cause of God in these parts. The whole work, however, has been carried on by God in so mysterious a manner, that it would be difficult for any one person to fix on any particular circumstance, and say, 'I am the instrument by which this work has been accomplished.' . . . We see the effect; each one rejoices in it; and yet no one can say how it has been wrought.

As I close I want you to think with me about these words of Carey. They are the words of a man who, as I have said earlier, is sometimes called 'the founder of modern missions'. More than that, they are the words of a man who knew God.

Try to imagine what moved this man. Was it self-aggrandizement? If so, Carey was disappointed. But he shows no disappointment in the words I have just quoted.

The plain, undeniable fact is that Carey was moved from the beginning by the awesomeness of the glory of God. Earlier we saw that this was his motive at the outset of his career as a missionary. We see here that he had not changed. The conviction deepened. It grew with the years. God is glorious indeed!

It is not hard to understand that God's glory was a great part of Carey's message. Look at his words again. They were written to his mission friends in England. There is a spirit about them that must have permeated the man. Do you think that he hid these things from his converts? Did he tell none of them that the work 'has been carried on by God'? Did he leave India to learn these things for herself? The thing is impossible. Nor would Carey have wanted to do it!

But Carey is gone. And the men that came after him

are gone also. The task is now ours. It no longer belongs to them. They have rested from their labours. It now belongs to us.

What shall we do with it? May God help us not to hesitate. If we love our Saviour let us seek to make Him known. Let us carry His character, His person, to 'the regions beyond.' Let us work the works of Him who sends us while it is day. Let us say on His behalf, 'Look unto me, and be ye saved, all the ends of the earth: *for I am God, and there is none else!*'

If we have but small confidence in ourselves, that is good. That is good indeed. And if we have other fears we will look them in the face knowing that God is greater than them all. The cause of God must prevail. And even if we must tremble as we work, we will say with Paul the missionary,

> Now unto him that is able to do exceeding abundantly above all that we ask or think, according to the power that worketh in us.
> *Unto him be glory in the church by Christ Jesus* throughout all ages, world without end. Amen. (Ephesians 3:20–21).